Like Saving Summer in a Jar

Like Saving Summer in a Jar

The Story of James "Jimmy" Mathis A Strawbridge Boy

Amy Mathis

ISBN: 1540508536
ISBN-13: 9781540508539
Library of Congress Control Number: 2017919705
CreateSpace Independent Publishing Platform
North Charleston, South Carolina

In memory of my Dad
James Oliver Mathis
February 4, 1937–July 21, 2015

For my Dad, our favorite Strawbridge boy.
For my daughter, Everette.
And for the Mathis family, especially Dad's Momma,
the grandmother I never knew.

Contents

Author's Note

As I set out on this journey to tell my father's story, I did not realize how therapeutic and cathartic it would be for me. Sometimes I wrote for days like a fiend. Other days, my own grief was so overpowering that I had to take a break from the tears. It took a long while to settle on a structure and which stories to share that would paint the picture I wanted of Dad and how I wanted him to be remembered. As I interviewed people who knew my father, the last question I always asked everyone was, "If you could describe James Mathis in three words, what would they be?" It was amazing to me how many people used the same words over and over. Words like *giving, smart, compassionate, funny, respectful.* If nothing else, Dad was consistent. We should all be so lucky to be remembered with those words. *Giving* was always the first word people mentioned. I am hopeful that if I have done my job right here in telling his story, you will be left with the same impression of my father and how he lived his life.

When I completed the first draft, I had my sister Debbie read what I had written. I wanted to make sure that I was giving honor and respect to Dad and to our family. I wanted to make sure I was getting it right. We realized that while we were both present at many, if not all, the events I talk about in this book, her memories were very different from mine. We chalked it up to our seven-year age difference. Perhaps her perspective of past events would, in fact, be very different. It also made us realize that a memoir is just that: the memories and perspective of the person who is telling the story. So those of you who read this and knew my dad or were part of some of the events I talk about in these pages may also remember things a bit differently. That's OK. What follow here are my memories. It's Dad's story but told through my lens of how I remember him, how I honor him.

Acknowledgments

I GUESS, IN a weird way, I need to thank a man I never met. His name was Chester Craig. He was a pastor at Bowie Methodist Church in the late 1940s. They say that sometimes people are put in your path for a reason. This man definitely had a major impact on our family and on my father's life. I doubt whether he knew it at the time, but if my father had never gone to live at the Strawbridge Home for Boys when he was thirteen, the direction of his life would have been very different. Fitting that a man of the Lord was put in my father's family path and that random crossing led my father to a life at the boys' home in his youth—and to a life of giving back and doing good work for others. Methodist Church lessons that he learned well.

I also need to thank my family for allowing me the time and giving me the latitude to set out on this journey to tell my father's story. Really, it's our family's story. The research and learning things I never knew about my father were cathartic and healing in a way I never realized possible. I spoke to people and read about people I had heard about my whole life—some I got to know for the first time; some I got to know better. Thank you all for sharing your stories with me.

Thanks to my mom. Behind every great man is an even greater woman. She allowed me to interview her during a very difficult time. Her grieving time. I think sharing the stories about Dad and their life together was a little bit healing for her, too. Maybe the next book will be about her. She does not yet realize her greatness. She, too, will leave a very strong mark on this world someday. And I do not think she has yet finished all her good work. She has so much strength and so much more to give. More than she knows.

Thanks to Nicole, my niece, for sharing her story about learning to cook the pig meat in just the right way. We are thankful she is a fast learner and loves to cook. Our family gatherings pay tribute to Dad with every breakfast we get to share. It's usually holidays filled with lots of traditions—eating pig meat is just part of it. Nicole told her story as part of her eulogy. I used some of her story to tell mine. She also put her creative talents to work and designed the concept for the cover of this book. Pop-Pop would be so honored and so very proud.

Thank you to Dad's brothers and sisters, who lent their memories to this story. It was their story, too. Dad was their fearless leader for a long time. I was not around in the beginning of his story, so I relied on their thoughts and perspectives about Dad in a way only they would know. I hope I have gotten their stories right and that I have been respectful of all they went through during a difficult time in their lives. A special thank-you to Uncle Bill, Dad's brother Billy. Billy was there at Strawbridge from the start. From day one. He provided anecdotes and stories as only he remembers them and only he could tell them.

Thanks to the church folks, the Hopkins buddies, the Board of Child Care colleagues; all of you know who you are, and I am grateful that you agreed to share your stories about Dad and how he touched your life.

Thank you to Trevion and Crystal for sharing their stories. So much courage for what you went through. Your intersection with Dad's life path was clearly meant to be. I think you know that, too.

Finally, thanks to Dad. Because of him, I am who I am. He was a teacher and a role model, and I learned from him. I only hope that I can carry on all the lessons. He taught the value of a dollar earned with hard work, the respect for family and traditions, and the need to be grateful for what you have. And if you have the slightest more than what you need, then you give to others. You pass it on. He also taught Everette, my daughter, his granddaughter. He taught her to build things. But mostly, he helped her build wonderful memories of the things they did together, which she will carry with her always. We will always cherish them, preserve them— kind of like they are in a jar and you can pull them out when you want them or need them.

Prologue

THIS IS NOT going to be the greatest story ever told. It is not the only story ever told of a man who came from humble beginnings and made certain choices that led him to do good things with his life. But it's my dad's story and our family story, and I felt it needed to be told. It needed to be documented so that others could maybe follow his example.

It may only mean something to our family. Maybe his Strawbridge "brothers" and extended family will be interested in the story. Perhaps the townspeople in his adopted home—Sykesville, Maryland—will have some interest and curiosity. My only hope is that it will lead someone else to make choices in his or her life to help others. I think our world needs a lot more people like that right now. My dad wasn't one of a kind, but by today's standards, he was one in a million. Maybe this story will inspire someone else, so maybe there will be two (or more) in a million.

On the day I decided to finally put thoughts to paper to document my dad's life and legacy, I really was not in any mood to make dinner for my family. So what, you ask? Well, this was unusual, as I love to cook. But on this particular day, I had a hankering for Chinese food. And, of course, as is customary with a Chinese meal, we got fortune cookies at the end of the meal. We do this thing in our family that when you read your fortune, you have to say at the end of it either "under the covers" or "in your pants." It's a silly thing. But it creates a whole new level of fun.

For example, I had recently read a fortune that said, "Our brightest blazes of gladness are commonly kindled by unexpected sparks," and then I added, "in your pants!" Makes you smile, right? Regardless of which line you choose, it usually makes you laugh. And Dad loved it. Always cracked him up. His laugh was memorable. He put his whole body into it. Belly laugh, bending over uncontrollably, slapping his knees. It was fun to make him laugh and watch him enjoy life.

So, on that particular night, after my fried rice and sweet and sour chicken, I read my fortune cookie message. It said, "At the end of each day, think 'What has this day brought me, and what have I given it?'" Seriously. This did not warrant our typical traditional response. How do you say "under the covers" or "in your pants" after a fortune that reads like that? Was this Dad sending a message from heaven? Did he know I was at this place mentally to start to document his life? Do you believe in signs? I always sort of did. And now that Dad has passed, I believe in them more than ever. I see them all the time. Whether they're real or imagined. It doesn't matter. For me this fortune cookie message was a clear sign.

I think Dad lived his life like that fortune every day. He was always asking, "What have I given it? Have I done all that I can?" I plan to give you some things to think about through the lessons he lived by and the lessons he taught me. He was a simple man. And yet, a great man, too. A man who paid it forward and lived life by a standard we should all strive to follow. The majority of us will definitely fall short. But even in trying to live a life as he lived his, our world, and those in it, would be a whole lot better off.

First Words

Do all the good you can, by all the means you can, in all the ways you can, in all the places you can, at all the times you can, to all the people you can, as long as you ever can.

—JOHN WESLEY

It's July 25, 2015. I can still smell the lingering aroma of our big family breakfast. It smelled like the kitchen of a diner with a short-order cook slapping down eggs and breakfast meats on a busy Saturday morning. When our entire family gets together, it's all about the food. We show our love through food—lots of food—sometimes to the detriment of our waistlines! Breakfast for us is never complete without pork sausage and homemade scrapple that comes from the butcher shop, Bullock's, located in Westminster, Maryland. It had become a tradition for almost every holiday and any time the whole family was together that Dad was in charge of the "pig meat." He always patiently hand patted each sausage patty so that it was exactly the size of a half dollar. Each patty was the same size. (The engineering principles he learned at Johns Hopkins University were applied to everything he did, including cooking sausage.) Each patty in the skillet was turned at precisely the right time so that the browning on both sides was always even.

Then came the cooking of the scrapple. Don't turn your nose up. The scrapple from Bullock's is like no other. I am not sure I ever want to know what is in it, but it is delicious. Especially when Dad made it. Each one-pound hunk of scrapple was sliced into exactly quarter-inch pieces (the engineer in the house again). Each sliced piece was then dipped in flour and placed in the sizzling grease in the frying pan. He never put too many pieces in the pan at once as you had to give them room to cook evenly and just right. And it was always just right. His favorite way to eat it was with apple butter. Spreading it thick—sweet and savory. Some in our family use ketchup on it. For me, just plain with my eggs and toast, thank you very much. The smells and sounds of the pig meat sizzling in the pan will forever bring memories of Dad and the comforts of family and home.

But on this particular July morning, breakfast was a little different. Today, Nicole, my niece and Dad's granddaughter, was going to be cooking the meat, exactly the way Dad had taught her. He had passed on the family tradition. And she had been eager to learn. He had taught her how to do each step on the Saturday morning of a family weekend to Massanutten Mountain in Virginia. It was a beautiful fall weekend in late September 2014 that our family decided to meet for a weekend getaway. I had rented a place so we all could stay in one spot. Everyone was there. Nicole took notes so she would be able to repeat the pig-meat cooking steps should the time ever come that Pop-Pop would not be there to supervise. Then, on Thanksgiving weekend in November of that same year, she pulled out her notes to see if she could recreate what she had learned months before. Pop-Pop was there to supervise each step as she worked through the process. She was realizing the importance of the patience part. You have to take it step by step. Getting it right takes time.

And, so it was on this morning, July 25, 2015, that Nicole was prepping for breakfast in the kitchen. Dad—Pop-Pop to her—was not there to show her the steps or to make sure each piece was cut exactly the right thickness. His guiding hands were not making sure that each piece was placed in the pan and that they were browned in the grease to perfection. She didn't have her notes because they were home in North Carolina in a safe place. She was in Maryland, going on memory and trying to make sure to follow each step. We were honoring Dad today. Nicole was doing her part by making the pig meat for breakfast.

As the pig meat was cooking, I wanted to share the thoughts that were swirling in my head with him. I wanted to get his opinion about what I was going to say that day. I always went to Dad for the big things, the big decisions in my life. He wasn't there to make sure I would get the facts right. I couldn't "test drive" my speech. I was trying to put words together that would make sense so everyone would know how wonderful and thoughtful and humble this man had been. All the memories were all jumbled up. For you see, today was the day of Dad's funeral. We had lost Dad on July 21. The past several days had been a blur, and we still couldn't believe we were going through all this without him. He wouldn't be there to guide us, to help Mom with all the little things he did for her, to entertain us, to make us laugh, to slice the ham, to cook the scrapple, to just fix it, just jiggle it, just do it. "It" was a lot of things—big and small—to so many people.

I remember sitting on the bed in Mom and Dad's bedroom wondering how I was ever going to get through this day. I had agreed to speak on behalf of our family and give a eulogy for Dad. What was I thinking? I couldn't keep two coherent thoughts in my head. The funeral was in an hour, and I was still trying to put the finishing touches on my notes to share Dad's life. I wanted to share our memories, his anecdotes, and his jokes with hundreds of very sad people who would be showing up that day to pay honor, respect, and tribute to this man I called Dad. How do you begin to share so much greatness about a person in five to ten minutes? And then I looked up. Looking for an answer. Looking to the heavens for help. Dad, can you hear me? Can you help me?

And there it was. It was hanging on the wall over the clock radio that he awoke to every morning. It was a plaque I had given him for Father's Day when I was fourteen. I knew this because the date I had given it to him was marked on the back. I had probably bought it at Leggett's Department Store in Westminster, Maryland, what seems like a hundred years ago. When I was fourteen, there was no local Hallmark store in Sykesville to buy that last-minute gift you needed for any given holiday or special event. I know when I gave him this gift years ago on the day we honor fathers, the message didn't carry nearly the weight that it did today. The poem on the wall decoration took on new meaning. Here is what it said:

"World's Best Dad"
A father's love gives
Strength to his sons, guidance
To his daughters and
Protection to his home

> He is the most important teacher
> In their lives, because of him
> His children see qualities
> They will always look for in others
> (Jean Kyler McManus, 1977)

Was this another sign? Why at that moment, sitting there on their bed, was I really seeing this for the first time? I think Dad was still trying to teach something and leave me with something important to remember. The title was certainly true. And the message, too. I think I will forever be hard-pressed to find the same qualities my father possessed in others. I can only hope that I, too, possess some of those qualities.

During the funeral week, there was such an outpouring of love and honor from the community and everyone who knew Dad. People were saying things like "He was so amazing," "So kind," "So humble," "A wonderful, warm, loving, funny, patient man," and "A gentleman." Many said, "They don't make them like Jim Mathis anymore."

All the things people were saying about Dad were true. I realized then that we all should strive to live our lives so that we are described and honored in the same way when we leave this world. They were wonderful things. Wouldn't you want someone saying things like that about you? Further, I realized then that future generations should know my father's story and try to emulate his character, follow in his example. I knew his story needed to be told, and I wanted to be the one to tell it.

As I had searched for the words to say to honor my father that day, the gift I had given to him for Father's Day so long ago said it best of all. But it also inspired me to want to say more about this man I called Dad. His life started out so ordinary—less than ordinary, actually—but the mark he left on this world was something extraordinary. He touched lives in ways we will never know. But for some of those who were lucky enough to cross his path and share their story, we do know the impact that he made. I want to share some of their stories, too. His life became intertwined with others. His life was not the only one that took a different direction than he ever expected. His life was meant to change the course of others' lives, too.

Most life stories have a very clear-cut beginning, middle, and end. As this is a memoir about my father, you know how it ends. But it doesn't have to end with the ending of a life. If you live your life right, it will carry on in those you touch and inspire. All of us have pretty much the same beginning. It's what we do in the middle that makes the difference. But for some of us, life's road takes different twists and turns—some good, some bad—and through no control of your own, you can end up in places you never thought were possible. My father's life was a little bit like that. At the age of twelve, the course of his life was changed forever. Family tragedy dictated a new course. At the age of thirteen, he went to live at the Strawbridge Home for Boys in Sykesville, Maryland. His life, the choices he would come to make, and those he would come to know in his new home would be forever influenced by the fact that fate had stepped in and landed him on the doorstep of this boys' home in December 1950. This is his story.

The Boy

You're never wrong to do the right thing.

—MARK TWAIN

**Oliver and Sarah Mathis with baby James.
Washington, DC, 1937.**

Oliver's Children

James Oliver Mathis, "Jimmy," was born on February 4, 1937 at the Columbia Women's Hospital in Washington, DC. Like that line from the Harry Chapin song "Cat's in the Cradle," he came into the world in the usual way. He just happened to be born post–Depression era and pre–World War II. The February day Dad was born was a cold winter day, but there was no snow on the ground. Good thing, as he hated snow and cold. But the irony was that Dad was always cold. I think he came into this world with the constant winter chill of February on him. It never went away.

He was the first-born son of Oliver Bennett Mathis and the former Sarah Jane Miles. Oliver and Sarah were from Escambia, Alabama, located down near the Gulf of Mexico, west of the panhandle of Florida. They had met at a dance in Mobile. Their "meet-cute" took place at the Battle House Hotel and Restaurant, the refurbished building that had been the Civil War headquarters for Andrew Jackson. *Meet-cute* is a term from 1940s films to describe when a romantic couple meets for the first time. Their eyes meet, and they just know their future is together. Oliver and Sarah's meeting may not have been that romantic. Oliver called her Sadie, a childhood nickname. Dad always referred to her as Sarah. Of course, he called her Momma.

Sarah was a very striking woman. In family pictures Dad shared, she always reminded me of a young Lauren Bacall. She was tall and slender. She had high cheekbones and fiery auburn hair. And Oliver could clean up pretty well, too. It wasn't often you saw him in a suit, but when you did, he looked like quite the Southern gentleman. It was customary at that time that courtships did not last long. They met. They married. They wanted to start a family.

Out on the town. Dad's cousin Dan Gibson Jr., Dad's mom Sarah, his aunt Amy, Dan's wife Mary, and Dad's father, Oliver. Circa late 1930s.

They moved to Washington, DC, seeking a better life. Oliver and Sarah had come north to our nation's capital to find work, find ways to make a living for the family they wanted to start. Times were still pretty tough in Alabama, and opportunities there were very limited. Oliver was a talented artist. However, to make money in those days following his passion would have been difficult. So he did what he could to make it work for his family. He worked odd jobs, handyman jobs, painted houses. At least he was still using a paintbrush.

He was an everyman—very creative—and he worked hard. He eventually found work with F. S. Gichner Iron Works Inc. in DC. F. S. Gichner Iron Works was the company that would later win the contracts to design and manufacture the iron fences that encircle numerous capital and federal buildings in the city. Oliver, known as Dad or Granddaddy to his family, held this steady job for a couple of years, and life in DC was pretty good for the Mathis clan. At least, for a little while.

Dad's parents would later produce five siblings for Jimmy—three brothers and two sisters. Two years after Jimmy, William, or Billy, was born, and a year after that came the first girl, Sara. She was named after Momma, but they changed the spelling by dropping the *h* at the end. The family then moved from DC to Bowie, Maryland. Bowie was a rural area then, similar to what they had left behind in Alabama. The new house, such as it was, was bigger for the growing family, and there was land to plant a garden and to have a farm. At the homestead in Bowie, three more siblings came along—Richard, Inez, and finally, the baby, Ronald, or Ronnie. There was a ten-year age gap between Jimmy, the oldest, and Ronnie, the baby.

As the family continued to grow, work became scarcer, and money was tight. There were more mouths to feed. The home in Bowie, Maryland, was pitiful at best. It did not have indoor plumbing, and there was very little heat during the cold winter months. The children would pile on blankets to stay warm at night. And Dad would always talk about how you did not want to have to go to the bathroom in the middle of the night and get out of the warm cocoon of heavy blankets in your bed. If you had to go, you held it, and you waited until morning to make the trek to the outhouse in freezing temperatures. That way, you only had to go outside once. Until the day he died, Dad always slept with lots of blankets—recreating that childhood cocoon for warmth and comfort.

I don't really remember the house in Bowie. I just have this vision of some wood shack like something you would see in the Appalachian Mountains. There were inch-wide gaps in the wood planks of the house so that cold air was always coming in, and an old coon dog was always sitting on the porch. I think the dog's name was Butch. This scene in my head was stereotypical of poor hillbillies. The house never got indoor plumbing. My mother would share stories of going there years later for holidays and having the same issue of having to "hold it" forever and not go to the bathroom until she got back home to Sykesville.

Though as a child, I might have thought going to Bowie was a cool adventure, somehow, I have blocked out any memories of visiting my grandfather at that house. No real memories of my own. Just lots of stories told over the years and ideas from pictures all connected somehow into this crazy place called Bowie. Any references to Bowie Dad shared were always overshadowed with jokes and snickers and the infamous outhouse stories. No matter how bad it may have been, Dad always shared his childhood years with us with a smile on his face and a wistful longing in his eyes.

While the family would be considered poor by today's standards and even by the standards back then, they always appeared to be happy. At least they always appeared that way in the pictures Dad shared with us of that time in his life. There was always work to be done. The family had a large garden, and their mom, Sarah, always asked the kids to pick something, water something, or clean something. Their days were filled with church, chores, and schoolwork. At that time the family was going to a Baptist church. The Christian roots started early and ran deep.

I recall that Dad could always be called on to quote a Bible verse or know who in the Bible was married to whom, who fathered whom, or who had betrayed whom. It wasn't that he was overly religious; it's just that his brain was an endless source of facts on any topic—some useful, some useless. However, church was a constant in their lives, and this early Christian foundation was the beginning of his ongoing servitude to others. His sense was that, although they had so little to offer, there was always someone less fortunate than they. The Golden Rule of "Do unto others as you would have them do unto you" was a constant rule in the Mathis household.

Sarah, Dad's mother, was the consummate homemaker and made every effort to make the best of a difficult living situation. She accepted her lot in life and was resolute. I get the sense that she just took life for what it was and wanted to raise her children to work hard, be grateful for what they had, and be respectful of others.

My aunt Sara shared a letter with me that her mother had written in 1949. She was writing to her sister Willie in Florida. I was struck by a passage in the letter. Though they had so little, Sarah was worried about sending any extra clothing from her family to her sister's family and how to get a package to Florida quickly. Clothing the boys had outgrown, even though they may have been worn and stained, could be used by their cousins. I believe Dad's sense of giving was taught at a very early age.

Oliver continued to work as a handyman and painter to make ends meet and put food on the table and a roof over their heads. Oliver was a stern man and a strong disciplinarian. Dad used to say when he and Billy got in trouble, Granddaddy would ask them to go pick their punishment. Choose their poison. It was usually a belt or a switch or a paddle.

Today, Granddaddy would definitely be locked up for child abuse. No doubt about it. I don't say that in a mean way. For that time, it was normal to discipline your children in this manner. Dad would say, "It worked!" Whatever you had done, you were never doing it again as you knew the consequence. He would also say that if you did decide to make a bad choice and do something bad, you hoped you were wearing your corduroy pants that day. At least the fabric was a little thicker, and the whooping wouldn't hurt as bad. I'm not sure what they did in the summertime. I guess when it was hot, you made sure you were making good choices, and you didn't do anything bad that would warrant punishment. Or I guess they just wore their corduroy pants all year long.

Dad was also raised with a sense of respect for authority and leadership. As the oldest, he was always called upon to set the example for his younger siblings. Jimmy was raised with a clear understanding of what was right and wrong. If you were asked to do something, you did it right the first time. The rules were pretty simple. Do it right, or don't do it at all. Do what you are told. Say "Thank you," "Please," and "Excuse me" a lot. Respect your mother, elders, and authority. Pray and be thankful for what you have. No questions, no complaints.

My sister and I didn't have a prayer. We were taught to live by the same rules. I am not saying our childhood was necessarily bad, but it was extremely rigid. Thinking back, though, it was actually pretty good. We just knew the boundaries and didn't cross them, or we knew the consequence. There were no gray areas. Yet while Dad and his siblings clearly had this set of rules to live by, he would also describe the shenanigans he and his brothers would get into. They were always playing pranks on one another and usually getting into trouble. I think Dad and Billy wore corduroy a lot.

Growing up in a time when you were expected to help everyone in the family and do your part—well, that was a lot of responsibility for a bunch of kids, and sometimes they just needed to cut loose. I remember the endless stories about working in the garden and hauling water to the house for cooking and bathing. There was always something that had to be done—household basics we take for granted today. But in the 1940s, everything you had to do usually took all day to do it.

We always referred to Dad's mom as, well, Dad's mom. We called her that since we never knew her personally, so she was never a Grandma or a Mum-Mum. However, what we did know was that she was a hardworking, gracious, proud Southern Christian woman. We only knew her through pictures and stories. But I envision her to have been a very strong woman. She had to be to put up with Oliver and six kids—more boys than girls. I think her strength was handed down through many generations of women who persevered through many hardships. Dad's mother's family had descended from strong lineage—mostly English, but some

Scottish and Irish mixed in. There is even a story from family members who have researched our genealogy that there is a connection to William Shakespeare. The family history has been traced back to 1625, when they lived on Stratford-upon-Avon in Yorkshire, England. So who knows if the Shakespeare part is true, but it makes for an interesting story.

When the family originally came over on the boat from England, they landed in Philadelphia. They eventually took up residence in Bucks County, Pennsylvania, just north of the city. I find it strange that I now live in that area, too. My ancestors began their roots in America in my backyard. They were the first Buckingham Quakers who started the parish in 1699.

Sarah's roots were deep, and faith and doing good were just part of the fabric of the family. I have this fantasy picture in my head of her in a soft cotton housedress with faded pink flowers, and she's working in the yard. She has on an apron tied at the waist. There would always be something cooking on the stove, always something to be washed. She would have a constant smile on her face. She would be humming a church hymn as she worked in the garden. Her children were her strength, her heart.

The kids would be in the garden early every day to help her. They would harvest the vegetables all morning. Then, come afternoon, they would sit under the shade of a tree and prepare to preserve their harvest. Dad would share stories of snapping green beans for days. He, Billy, and Sara would make it a game. Who could fill a bowl the fastest? He would show us how to snap the ends, then snap the beans in half to get them ready to be canned. By the end of the day, their hands were green, too, from the beans. Their hands smelled like dirt, like the earth. Good, wholesome, hard work. This was how they spent their summers. Every summer.

They say everything you need to know in life you learn before you are in kindergarten. If that is true, then Sarah is the one responsible for teaching Dad all that he was in life. She taught him to be honest and gracious. Life would take a hard, twisted turn for their family, and it would certainly have an impact on Dad and his siblings. I think she was a big part of the reason he became the man he was.

Although the life was tough compared to life today, it was just life as usual for rural families at that time. The movie that plays in my head about life in the Mathis house in Bowie is part *O Brother, Where Art Thou?* and part *Deliverance*. I think Dad's mother, Sarah, did the best she could with what she had to work with. I believe there was a lot of love in their house. And I get the sense that they didn't know there was any other type of life to live. Everyone they knew was living the same hardscrabble life.

The work in the garden was a necessity. There were always tomatoes, cucumbers, beans, and corn growing in the dirt. The hot summers were spent making sure something grew so that there would be something to eat in the winter. There was always something to grow, something to pick, something else to plant. They wanted to save summer in a jar. Dad would share stories of the pantry his mom kept and how it always seemed full. Life was hard, but they had what they needed. They were happy and healthy, and they made the best of it.

Then in 1949, life as they knew it came to a halt. On April 11 of that year, Sarah, their mother, had been working in the kitchen. This was her normal post for midday. She had been opening cans of food to prepare meals for the day. Just outside the pantry, there was a wall-mounted can opener. It had a long metal piece that you pulled out to hold the can in place, and then you turned a crank manually to open the lid off the can. This metal piece needed to be put back up in place when you were done opening a can. However, for some reason on that day, the metal piece did not get put back.

Later, as Sarah was working in the kitchen and heading back and forth from the pantry, she walked right into the metal piece and hit her head.

Hard. The very next day, April 12, she dropped dead suddenly in the kitchen from a massive head injury. It was baby Ronnie's second birthday; Sarah was just thirty-nine years old. She literally never knew what had hit her. And neither did Oliver or the children.

Divine Intervention

The summer of 1949 without their mother was quite different for Dad and his siblings. Uncle Bill said they called it the "summer of discontent." I can't imagine how my grandfather handled it. Trying to keep some sort of normalcy for himself and his six kids. But nothing was normal. Oliver was lost without his Sadie. I am not sure if my grandfather ever recovered from the grief of losing her.

The man I remember was a very heavy smoker and an even heavier drinker. Whiskey, preferably Wild Turkey bourbon, was his drink of choice. Though I am not sure he cared what he drank, as long as it was something with some alcohol content. He was known to make his own dandelion wine. Dad used to say you could use it to strip paint off a car. Or, at the very least, set your hair of fire. I have a vague recollection from when I was little—Granddaddy would come to visit our house, and he would keep a bottle of something under his pillow. Well, actually, it was my pillow, as he would sleep in my room.

Mom was always worried he would drop ashes from his cigarettes on the wood floors or burn holes in the furniture. I am sure he did that more than once. He would let cigarettes burn down to the nub (no filters as he rolled his own) and then light the next one with what was left of the previous one. Dad would say if you looked up *chain-smoker* in the dictionary, there would be a picture of Granddaddy.

Dad used to also tell this story of how Granddaddy could go into places that did not allow smoking and roll up the cigarette in his mouth, still lit. Then, when he went back outside, he would roll it back out, and it was still lit. I am not certain that story is true, but at the time, it sounded like a really cool trick. As a kid, I would get this cartoon picture in my head of smoke coming out of his ears. How did he do that? But, please, don't try it at home. Sorry. I digressed from the story.

Oliver did love his kids. He continued to make sure that church was a part of their lives. He was not able to care for them quite the way that Sarah had, but he was doing the best he could. He tried to make sure that the daily routines his Sadie had in place for them were still there to rely on. But he still had to work. The children were left home alone with a revolving door of church ladies and housekeepers to care for them during the day. It was actually the local church that eventually stepped in to help Oliver and provide a possible solution to help raise his family. I think the church ladies realized that Oliver was overwhelmed and the kids needed care and supervision.

I often think about the story Dad would tell about the months that followed the death of their mother. He recalled that they would be hungry and were only eating whatever Oliver could scrape together for them. His go-to meal was something they called "chili-mac." It was a can of chili poured over noodles. However, the pantry was still full of all the canned vegetables from the summer before. The jars were labeled and stacked in neat rows on the pantry shelves just gathering dust. Vegetables they had picked and canned. The harvest she had grown and sown. Oliver would not let anyone touch them. Not one jar was out of place. I think he felt the jars represented a piece of her he wanted to preserve, just like what was inside.

I think he saw his children in the same way. They were a piece of her. He needed to make sure he preserved them and provided them with a home that would allow them to grow and prosper, just like the vegetables in the garden. He needed to tend to them. It's what she would have wanted and what she would have expected. Somehow, I think in Oliver's mind, they, too, had become like summer in a jar. Something he needed to save.

The local Baptist church the family attended had become Bowie United Methodist Church. The church gave Oliver a suggestion and a possible new direction for his family. In 1948, the Baptist church in Bowie became part of the Methodist Church Conference (also part of the Baltimore-Washington Conference). In the early 1920s, it was this Conference of Methodist Churches that had become the benefactor of a farm in Carroll County, Maryland. At that time, the wish of the deceased owner, George Albaugh, was to turn the farm into a home for underprivileged boys to fulfill a social service need for local families.

The Albaugh family had been faced with a need to care for children due to the loss of their parents, and at that time, they were offered limited choices. George Albaugh's brother and his wife had perished in an influenza outbreak and left three boys to be raised by the family. Social services and support agencies were not readily available, especially in rural areas. The family did not want other families to face similar hardship and have to make difficult decisions for the care of their children in a crisis.

The idea came to them to establish a boys' home. The family farm was offered to the church as possible refuge for families in need. It was known as the Strawbridge Home for Boys and originally opened in 1924.

By the summer of 1950, many boys had passed through the halls of Strawbridge—lived there, played there, and called it home. It was that summer of 1950 that the pastor of the Bowie Methodist Church, Pastor Chester Craig, was put in the Mathis family's path. This was a pivotal turning point for the family. Choices made at this point in time forever changed the direction of the family. I have always wondered what led my grandfather to that point. What led him to the church for direction? How did the conversation go between him and the pastor? What about the family back in Alabama? Couldn't the family have stepped in to help raise Dad and his siblings?

Apparently, some of the family did step in. Jimmy, Billy, Sara, and Richard were older, and so the sentiment was that they did not need much more raising or guidance. But Inez and Ronnie were still babies. Dad's aunt Amy, and her husband, Bill, were coming to Maryland. Dad's uncle Bill was in the navy, and he was going to be stationed in Annapolis, Maryland, for a period of time to work at the Naval Academy. They offered to take in Inez and Ronnie. It is my understanding that they kept my aunt and uncle for almost two years and would have perhaps adopted them as their own. But, as fate would have it, Uncle Bill received new orders from the navy, and they were shipped out to Japan.

My grandfather still needed to determine how to care for his older children and figure out what would be best for all of them, including Inez and Ronnie. The church ladies who were helping the family suggested that he speak to the local pastor. The church had homes for children in need. Perhaps it could be an option to help his family. It's hard to know how my grandfather arrived at the answers. I am sure it was not easy for him to think about sending his children away from the only home they ever knew. Sometime in the fall of 1950, my grandfather went to meet with Pastor Craig at the Methodist church.

Who knows how the conversation went or what was really said? To this day, I don't know how any parent, let alone my grandfather, would be able to do this most unselfish act. I guess it would be similar to giving your children up for adoption with only the children's well-being in mind. You would do it so that they could have a better life than you could ever give them. The details of this time are a bit sketchy. I am not sure if my grandfather had a choice to give up his children or if he made the most sacrificial choice. He had lost his wife and now was planning to give up his children. His children had lost their mother, and now, their father was considering placing them in someone else's care.

For a large portion of their lives, they would be living away from him. He would still get to see them a few times a year, but for the most part, they would live under another roof and be raised by others. And so my grandfather took Pastor Craig's suggestion, and on December 8, 1950 (yes, right before Christmas), Dad and his brother Billy took the long ride from Bowie, Maryland, to Sykesville, Maryland. They were headed to the Strawbridge Home for Boys.

The home was only for boys ranging in ages from six to eighteen. So Sara and Richard were taken to another home run by the church in Washington, DC. It was called the Swartzell Children's Home. Eventually, Inez and Ronnie would join them at this home. Their mother had been gone more than a year, and now the family was divided. Dad and his siblings were living in separate homes.

I often wonder what the conversation was like in the car among Granddaddy, Dad, and Uncle Bill as they drove out to their new home. They rumbled out to Carroll County in a 1949 Hudson Terraplane. Dad's brother Richard said the car was gray. Well, supposed to be gray. Mom remembers it was just rust colored. Maybe Granddaddy needed to use some dandelion wine on it. Oliver didn't always take the best care of his cars. He just kept them filled with gas and oil. Maybe it was a good idea that he was making sure his kids would be cared for a little better than his cars. As the miles went by, what was going through their minds? Fear, anxiety, excitement—lots of emotions all worked up into lots of questions.

And what was going through Oliver's mind? How could he explain all the unknowns to them? He didn't really have the answers. What was this new place? Who were these people who would raise his children? And how would any answer be acceptable for Jimmy and Billy to agree that is was all going to be better? How was this going to make it right?

It is still so hard to believe that this was to become the fate of my father's family. The way Dad told the story, they were actually grateful to have a better place to go, a better place to live. They would have heat and indoor plumbing. Who knew you could go to the bathroom inside? The home was offering "three hots and a cot"—three square meals a day and a warm bed. And really, it was offering a whole lot more than that. But on that dreadful day in December, my grandfather had to leave them on the doorstep of this strange place.

They were starting a new life—new place, new school, new people, new rules. My father was just a young boy. He was only thirteen. His brothers and sisters were even younger. But as the oldest, he was their leader. They were looking to him to see how he was handling this new family situation. How, at thirteen years old, do you handle the fear of all these new unknowns? And what if, just a year ago, you had lost your mother? I think about how scared he must have been. But he couldn't let them see that. This new life was thrust upon them, and he had to be strong for them. This early impression of him by his family lasted his whole life. He was always their go-to, the consummate leader of the family.

Oliver and his children (left to right)—Billy, Richard, Sara, Ronnie on Oliver's lap, Inez, and Jimmy. April 1949.

This Place Called Strawbridge

The Strawbridge Home for Boys was located off Old Sykesville Road, now known as Maryland Route 32. The Baltimore-Wilmington Conference for Methodist Churches (now known as the Baltimore-Washington Conference) had inherited the property of the old Manro Farm owned by the Albaugh family. Mr. and Mrs. George Albaugh had given the land to the church with the instruction and intention to build a home for boys. The Methodist Church already had two other similar children's homes—the Kelso Home for Girls and the Swartzell Children's Home. Those two homes were located in Washington, DC.

The Albaugh family had donated the farmland and buildings on the property. The boys' home was originally dedicated at a ceremony in 1922. The house and barns were repurposed and opened as a home for boys in 1924. The vision of the Albaugh family to offer a home and services to children became known as the Strawbridge Home for Boys, and its mission and purpose were dedicated to the protection, training, and development of young boys in need in the Baltimore and Wilmington Conferences of the Methodist Church. The home was named after Robert Strawbridge. He had been a pioneer circuit rider and the first Methodist pastor in Carroll County, Maryland.

The Reverend Thomas Long was named the first superintendent on December 16, 1924. On that same day, the first fifteen boys moved in to become the very first residents, along with two housemothers to care for them. The boys called the building they lived in "the Strawbridge Cottage."

In 1927, the Carroll Building was the first new building built on the property, and a superintendent's cottage was built around the same time. Inside the Carroll Building, there were two dormitories for the boys. Each dorm had a housemother, and eventually, they had housefathers, too. The boys were given the basics of life—food, shelter, and clothing. In addition, they also attended the local schools. Depending on the age of the boys, they attended either Mechanicsville Elementary School, which had grades one through six, or Sykesville School, which had grades six through twelve. For religious training the boys attended St. Paul's United Methodist Church on Main Street in Sykesville, Maryland. The first three pews on the right were always reserved for the boys. Today, they are still referred to as "the Strawbridge pews" by the church members.

The boys who came to live at Strawbridge were either orphans, having lost both parents, or had only one parent at home to attempt to care for them. Hard choices were made by their families or for their families so the children could have better lives. Those with some type of family unit were able to visit their families on holidays. They could also visit family for a few weeks during the summer months. Those who did not have family to go to were temporarily taken in by local families who volunteered their homes much like foster families do today. A part of the Strawbridge mission was to make sure the boys always felt they were part of a family.

By 1950, several hundred boys had lived at the home. On that cold December morning in 1950, a few weeks before Christmas, two Mathis boys were about to make their mark on Strawbridge history. At this point, Reverend Holmes Lockhardt was the superintendent of the home. He was a stern, righteous man, something Jimmy and Billy were already used to with their own father. The story we always got about that fateful day they were taken to Strawbridge was that they felt like they had died and gone to heaven. It was almost like Shangri-la. The home had heat and indoor plumbing. Who knew you could have such luxuries in your home? Three meals were served daily. And they instantly had forty more brothers! Not blood brothers—more like a band of brothers. Brothers by circumstance.

While it seemed that life was getting better for them, I still find it hard to believe that those first few weeks and months were a walk in the park for Oliver's children. It was probably a very tough transition time. Yes, some things might have been surprisingly better, but they had left their siblings behind for something unknown. Oliver may have been a tough father, but he was still their father and provided what he could. He was the only father they had known. He had tried to work out ways to raise his family and carve out a living. The Strawbridge Home for Boys and the church-managed homes in Washington, DC, had offered options for his two oldest boys and their younger siblings that he would never have been able to provide them.

When my dad would talk about that time in their lives, he was always very thankful, always forever grateful. This was the beginning of a mind-set he would carry with him for the rest of his life. It's that old question of nurture versus nature. I think Dad was born with a sense of caring and kindness. He had an innate sense of right and wrong and a strong sense of leadership. Through the structure provided at the home and through the care of Miss Alice Seymour, his housemother, I think he was also nurtured to develop those innate abilities beyond his normal, natural scope. His momma had built the foundation; Strawbridge built on that and took it to a whole new level.

Jimmy and Billy were roommates in the Carroll Building. As Dad was older, he would eventually move on to the Memorial Cottage for the older boys. But at least for the first year or so, he and Billy remained together. There were four boys to a room. So much for any privacy. Life wasn't much different at Strawbridge than life at home in Bowie. Same brother for a roommate, same hard work expected. The boys worked on the farm, did their homework, and went to church. There was structure and discipline and expectation. My father thrived in this environment. He had been the leader of his siblings and was always doing what his momma asked of him. It was not hard for him to follow the rules at this new home. His brother Billy, however, had some challenges, but that's a whole other story. (A sequel, perhaps?) Dad, as the oldest, always looked out for his little brother. Despite all their new extra brothers, blood was still thicker. Uncle Bill recalls that Dad was always seen as a leader, a protector.

Dad (standing, fifth from the right), his brother Billy (standing, sixth from the right), and some of their other "brothers" in front of the Carroll Building at Strawbridge. Circa early 1950s.

The Strawbridge Home for Boys was a working farm. There were cows, chickens, hogs, and horses. There was a vegetable garden. It was just so much bigger than what their momma had had in Bowie. Dad would always say that the cows didn't know what day it was, even if it was a holiday or summertime. And they certainly could not tell time. They just knew they were hungry and still needed to be fed twice a day no matter what.

**The barns, sheds, out-buildings, and pool at
the Strawbridge Home for Boys.**

The boys would have to feed the animals before going to school, and there were chores and homework to do when they got home. There was ease in the monotony of the daily routine. They always say that children like schedules and limits. I am not sure all children believe that, but Dad learned the lessons well. Even today, I live by a schedule and the to-do list. Dad's lessons were passed on. It's a blessing or a curse. I am not sure sometimes.

The housemothers and housefathers became surrogate parents to the boys. Dad lost his mother when he was so young, and I think he latched onto his housemother, Miss Alice Seymour. He had such a fondness for her. As Dad would describe her to us, I would imagine that she took care of their hurts and consoled them when they had bad dreams. She read to them at night. She tucked them in. She made them say their prayers. She checked their homework. She made them eat their green vegetables. She was proud of their achievements at school and in sports. And she did it for so many boys, for so many years. Just like a mother would. They were her boys.

There was also a housefather. Dad's housefather was Mr. Archie Horn. And apparently, he loved Dad. In later years, he would entrust Dad with the home's station wagon and let Dad drive the boys to various outside activities. I picture that the car looked like the Clark Griswold mobile from the movie *Vacation*—an ugly shade of green with wood panels. We always compared Dad to Clark—maybe this was how it all started.

Dad would drive the boys to the Ambassador Movie Theater near Gwynn Oak Junction, just outside Baltimore. They probably went to see the movies of the day, such as *Rear Window* with Jimmy Stewart or *On the Waterfront* with Marlon Brando. He would also take them bowling in Sykesville. The bowling alley was in a building next to the fire station on Main Street. I remember going there to play as a kid. There was a man whose job was to set up the pins. Manually. Funny to think of that now. My daughter and I recently went bowling, and I shared that story with her. She was like, "Geez, Mom, part of the fun is all the noise and lights blinking as the pins get knocked down and set up!" How did we think it was fun to watch a man do the same thing by hand? I couldn't answer. I think back then we just set the "fun" bar of expectation a lot lower.

The fact that Mr. Horn let Dad drive the car was a big deal. He didn't allow any of the other boys to do things like that. Descriptions of Mr. Horn ranged from strict to very strict, and he did not put up with any excuses. I am guessing Dad was able to get along with him pretty well as Mr. Horn sounded a bit like his own father, and Dad was used to treating his authority figures with respect. It's how his momma raised him. Strawbridge wasn't just called a home. It had become his home.

Asparagus Butts

I can't imagine mealtimes at the home. How do you feed that many grow-ing boys at one time? How many gallons of milk did they have to get out of those cows every morning? I picture a free-for-all in the dining area. And it's very loud, and it's chaos, and it's crazy. It's like the food fight scene in *Animal House*. And I would be very wrong. The boys had to be respectful and mind their manners. There was always a prayer before the meal. You had to be thankful for whatever was put in front of you to eat. You might not like it, but it didn't matter. There were no other choices hiding in the kitchen pantry that they would whip up just for you. The cook was not preparing different options for every taste bud. There was no gluten-free, no fat-free, no worry about food allergies. Most of what they were eating had come from the farm or had been donated by generous local churches and communities.

By the time the boys would come in for breakfast, they had already been out working with the animals on the farm. They had milked the cows and fed the sheep, the horses, and the hogs. They had bathed, combed their hair, brushed their teeth, and dressed for the day.

Dad (on the far right) and some of his Strawbridge brothers getting ready for school. Early 1950s.

Today, I have a constant fight with my daughter every morning just to get her to brush her teeth. Let's not talk about the hair. I need lessons from Miss Seymour on how she got forty boys to do this every morning. At the home they did not put up with any foolishness, and the boys were responsible for their own personal hygiene and care. They started each day with making their beds the minute they were out of them, a lesson I learned from Dad and still do today. I can't start the day without first making the bed. I realized years later that it was not just about being neat; it was about discipline and good habits you form that you do every day.

If you don't do anything else in the day, make your bed. You can say with confidence that you have at least accomplished one thing on your to-do list for the day. I realize there are people who do not live with a running list of things to do every day. I don't know how they function.

Lunch would be packed for the boys, or they could get lunch at school. By dinnertime the boys would be ravenous from a long day at school. Keep in mind, after school there was homework to do and chores to be done on the farm. Suppertime would be a repeat of breakfast. Different food, of course. But there was always meat and two or three sides. Milk to drink. The dining ritual would include knowing what utensils to use, or you were taught if you had not learned this lesson prior to coming to Strawbridge. Napkins went in your lap and were used to wipe your face and hands as you ate. Yes, the boys were taught that napkins serve a purpose. Not just to make slingshots or wear as a headband or eye patch like a pirate! Although my uncle did not learn this lesson too well.

There were prayers to thank the Lord for the good food you were about to receive and to bless those hands that had prepared it. At Strawbridge those hands belonged to Mr. Jackson, the head cook in the kitchen. He was thanked every day, and he truly had blessed hands for the work he was doing to feed those boys. I am certain he was not getting five-star reviews from Zagat, but he was feeding fifty people a day, three times a day. He deserved to be the top chef of the day! I am sure Bobby Flay or Gordon Ramsay could not have done a better job feeding all those hungry bellies of growing boys.

Years later, these table rituals were also taught in my house. My dad did not want any nonsense at the table. You were there to eat and share stories of the day. No telephone interruptions. No TV. Keep in mind that in those days, the telephone did not have an answering machine. There were only three options—it rang forever, it was busy if you were on it, or someone answered it. There certainly were no games or gadgets or devices at the table. If the telephone rang during dinner, Dad would say, "If it's important, they will call us back." And you know what? They did.

Your plate always had some kind of meat and two sides. And no meal was complete without applesauce. I'm not kidding. If you haven't tried it, you do not know the value of a good forkful of something you do not like dipped in applesauce. Ketchup can also be a good substitute. You can mask the awful chalk flavor of liver or make a good dip for yucky-tasting veggies like brussels sprouts or lima beans.

Dad would always tell the story of his introduction to one of my favorite vegetables, asparagus. Asparagus is definitely an acquired taste. As you most likely are aware, this green stalk-like vegetable only grows in the spring. It has a very short harvest season and can be so yummy prepared in a variety of ways—grilled, steamed, sautéed with garlic, in a casserole or salad. Once the stalks are ripe and ready to eat, you cut them from the garden, wash them up, and snap off the ends. When you are snapping the stalk, it will always break just where the tender part meets the tough part. My dad never knew there was a tender part! He never acquired the taste.

Since nothing was ever thrown away at Strawbridge that could provide any part of the meal, the tough part of the asparagus stalk was cooked up, too, and served to the boys. It wasn't until years later that Dad found out about the tender part. Until then he was just eating asparagus as it was served to him. The butt ends were boiled up but never got tender. I'm sure if he had the chance, he dipped them in applesauce or ketchup. You just had to clean your plate, or there was trouble from Miss Seymour.

Upon discovery of the tender part of asparagus, Dad used to refer to the parts they were given at Strawbridge as "asparagus butts." There are probably some Strawbridge boys who to this day have never learned to appreciate this vegetable and still think you only eat the butt ends.

Dad learned the lesson that food was never wasted. I do have to say that I think my feelings about leftovers today are deeply rooted in the fact that growing up, we ate the same meal for days. Today, I rarely cook the same thing twice. And I hate leftovers. But my father loved them, and my guess is that he got pretty creative with suggestions to my mother on new ways to prepare something. For example, roasted chicken on day one became chicken and dumplings on day two. Then it turned into chicken a la Jimmy on day three (don't ask!), and by day four, the chicken bones went into chicken soup. A week later, you were probably still eating soup from that same chicken. He learned how to stretch a good piece of meat. Sometimes it was just stretched too far.

I am not sure if it was the teachings from his momma and daddy from the South or Mr. Jackson, the cook, but there were parts of animals my father would eat that you just do not want to know about. I remember as a little girl going to Will's butcher shop with Dad on a Saturday morning and seeing the strangest things. Tripe, souse, pickled pigs' feet. Dad would talk about eating hog's ass and hominy. I used to think it was a joke. But after too many trips to the butcher, I think Dad actually ate hog's ass. No, I know he did. It's funny that my husband, who is from Kyrgyzstan, is also very familiar with these strange culinary delights. No part of an animal is ever wasted or trashed. My father and my husband had those eating habits in common.

This also stood true for leftovers and the mystery things you would find in our refrigerator days later after a big meal. Dad would always say he had an iron stomach. He would eat fried souse (what is in that stuff anyway?) and pickled pigs' feet. Lunch meat could be in the fridge for weeks with rainbows on it, and he would say something like "Fry it up—will kill what's on it and taste better anyway." I do think it's a Southern thing—anything pigs and anything fried. I sometimes wonder if he just said things like that to be funny or if it was because of the way he was raised.

I know there were times after his mother had passed away that Dad and his brothers and sisters were hard-pressed to find anything to eat. They would eat whatever they could scrounge up or find in the fridge. Parents are always saying something to their kids about the starving kids in Africa. For my father, I think it was about the starving kids in Bowie. He would eat whatever was put in front of him. No complaints. He was always a member of the clean-plate club. But he always kept two Tums on his bedside table. I think he realized years later his stomach wasn't made of iron after all.

Summer at Strawbridge

Thanksgiving, Christmas, Easter, and two weeks in the summer were family time. The boys who had a parent or family to visit were able to go home during these holidays and spend that time with their families. Dad would get to go home and see his father and the rest of his brothers and sisters. This unique living arrangement allowed Dad to maintain a relationship with his father and spend time with his siblings. It was a time to reconnect and make sure they remained a close family. Many years after Strawbridge and until the day he died, Dad always kept the family together and connected. He was always reaching out to his brothers and sisters on holidays and birthdays or special occasions. Until he died, he spoke to his brothers every week. They shared a special bond. If you were to ask them now, it's these weekly calls that they miss so much. It was how they stayed close. He was the glue that held them all together—when they were children and through the rest of their lives.

Jimmy had fallen into the regimens and routines of Strawbridge. He excelled in school. He followed the rules, and he was liked by whomever he met, at school, at church, and at the home. Summertime meant there was no school, but the work on the farm at Strawbridge continued. There was always something to do. When the boys were not working, there were opportunities to play ball—baseball, basketball, or dodgeball.

There was also a pool on the Strawbridge property for the boys to cool off when the heat of the work would make them almost pass out. But, as Dad told it, it's surprising that the boys didn't develop hypothermia. It was a cement pool fed by a spring, and the water was so cold you would turn blue if you were in it for more than a minute. Dad would say that it felt great to jump in and it would definitely cool you off, but you would jump out just as fast. And it was deep. Always felt like you were jumping into a quarry instead of a pool. There are stories of snakes, and Lord knows what else was at the bottom. There were no frills like at community pools today. No pool toys, no umbrellas, no lounge chairs. Just a hard, concrete pool. They would make up their own games. Mostly to get warm again after that first dip, get hot, jump in, turn blue, get out, and repeat.

Summertime also meant the chance to go home again for two weeks. For Dad and his family, going home would have meant heading back to Bowie. It was also the chance to head south to Pensacola, Florida, and Alabama to spend time with their Grandmother Mathis and other family members and get to play with their cousins. It was like their summer camp. Their father would make the drive out to Sykesville to pick them up at Strawbridge. Then, the next day, Granddaddy would go get Sara and Richard from the home in Washington, DC. They were old enough to make the trip south. Then all of them would take the long train ride from Washington, DC, to Florida.

The trip would take several days and was quite an adventure. They would survive on hard-boiled eggs and fried chicken. Dad would always talk about how, by the third day, the eggs and chicken would smell pretty ripe, and I'm sure the other passengers on the train really enjoyed it. He thought it was so funny that they were stinking up the train. Sara remembers having to fight her brothers to get any of the food. She now wonders why she fought so hard, since it probably tasted pretty bad and wasn't worth the fight.

As Dad recalled these summer trips, he would ask, "What do you think came first? The stinky chickens or the stinky eggs?" He swore you could keep hard-boiled eggs for a week or more—unrefrigerated. I'm not sure about that. But I think they tested that theory every summer on the train ride to Florida. As Uncle Bill tells it, I'm not sure what smelled worse—the eggs going in as they ate them or the foul-smelling gases coming out their butts after. Stale eggs, stale sandwiches, and boys playing a game of What's That Smell? Poor sister Sara. It was kind of like the road-trip game the cartoon characters Bart and his dad, Homer, would play on the TV show *The Simpsons*.

The southbound train made stops at every station along the way. Their train was not the Amtrak Express Acela. On the trip to Florida, there was always a stop in Birmingham, Alabama. It was always a little bit longer than the other stops, and they could get off the train to stretch and walk around. On one particular trip, Dad's brother Billy did not get back on the train when it left the Birmingham station headed for the last stop at Pensacola, Florida. They got all the way to the last stop and realized Billy was not on board. He had gone off on his own adventure at the Birmingham train station. Dad, always the leader and the organizer, made sure they went back to get him.

I'm not sure of the details on that, but regardless of whether they went back to get him by train or car, it would have cost extra to make that extra trip. I am also certain that Grandmother Mathis would not have been too happy about the wasted money and wasted time. Given what I know of her from stories and the little I remember of my grandfather, I am sure they would have just made Billy walk the 250 miles to Pensacola. That would have taught him a lesson he would never forget. I wonder if Billy was wearing corduroy pants that day.

Once they got to Florida, though, Grandmother Mathis had her hands full with six more kids added to her care. It was a week of playing games with their cousins and spending time with family. Imaginary battles, team sports games, chasing the dogs (hound dogs, I am sure), playing hide-and-seek. Lots of fun times with cousins.

Grandma Mathis had a big tree in the front yard with a tire swing. They would play Tarzan until dark, and then they would chase fireflies. They would catch them and put them in mason jars or old jelly jars with holes poked in the tops so they would at least survive until morning. They would be natural night-lights with their blinking yellow light. The children would always add some sticks and grass to the jar so the fireflies thought they were still outside. The bugs couldn't tell you, but I am pretty sure they knew the difference. But again, this notion of trying to preserve things.

Apparently, Grandma Mathis was quite the adventurer, and she made sure the children had lots of adventures and used their imaginations. She definitely did not fit the mold for women of her era. She got bitten by the gold-rush bug, and there are pictures of her panning for gold out west. I don't think she was going to get rich on the gold she found, but I'm sure she had fun trying. In the same box of old pictures were photos of her hiking in the mountains and jumping waves in an ocean. She marched to the beat of a different drum. I think that her fearless nature and attitude for grabbing life with both hands rubbed off on Oliver's children each summer they spent with her. Good attributes to inherit.

It seems that Grandmother Mathis had her own imagination and knack for storytelling. Perhaps it started as bedtime stories for some of the young Mathis boys wanting more adventure. There is an infamous urban legend that Dad's Mathis side of the family descended from the Poarch band of Creek Indians, who had settled in Alabama. Dad was always telling us the story of how we were part Native American Indian. I think I even wrote a paper about when I was in middle school. The story went so far as to include that the family owned land that had been part of an Indian reservation. It's funny that this story has been passed around and told for years with new embellishments each time. We only found out recently that it was just that—a story.

Grandma Mathis was a woman of many talents. She told exaggerated stories the children loved. And the love of good food was ingrained early. She could cook. Good Southern-style cooking. Dad would reminisce about the smell of cornbread browning in an iron skillet, pots of beans or soup always on the stove, collard greens, and black-eyed peas. Dad loved these foods. He grew up with them. They were comfort foods. And there were always homemade pies. Grandma Mathis always put her pies on the kitchen windowsill to cool. Sounds like something from a Norman Rockwell painting. I do not think Pensacola was that idyllic, but I do think that she loved those kids with her whole heart. She loved when they came to visit. I think after they had lost their momma, she always had a soft spot for them and wanted them to know they had a family who cared.

They also got to spend time with their momma's family. Aunt Willie and her children were nearby. I always thought it was strange that Dad's aunts all had names that were typically male names—Aunt Willie, Aunt Jimmie, and even an Aunt Oscar. Her name was Oscar Amelia. Dad said it was because their father had wanted boys who would be able to work on the farm. I always thought that was terrible. The girls could work the farm just as easily with names like Mary, Anne, or Elizabeth. Dad just said it was the crazy South. That's what they did.

As the story goes, one time Grandmother Mathis had put an apple pie on the sill to cool. Dad and the other boys were out in the yard playing games and could instantly smell the aroma of the freshly made pie. Nothing better than the smell of an apple pie hot out of the oven. They were in the bushes playing some form of war game like Take the Hill or something to that effect. Dad was the oldest, so he volunteered, or it was volunteered for him, that he would sneak up through the yard and take the pie off the windowsill. The pie was some kind of treasure behind enemy lines to be captured or saved or, at the very least, eaten.

Jimmy was slinking across the yard on his belly. Slithering like a snake and being so careful not to make a noise or get caught, he reached his target—the window—and stood up to get the prize (the pie). At that moment, he did not know that the general of their enemy—his grandmother—had known their strategy. He did not know what hit him. Just beyond the shadows, standing in the window, was his grandmother with an iron frying pan in her hand, and she coldcocked him right on the head. Dad's brothers were still hiding in the bushes, and they saw the whole thing happen.

As my uncle tells the rest of the story, Dad literally fell straight backward. He was just like a fallen soldier in the trenches. Once they were done laughing, his brothers came out of hiding to drag him back to the bushes. With no pie. But he did come back with a very large lump in the middle of his forehead. I am not sure if Grandmother Mathis was smart or crazy—maybe a little of both. The frying-pan-to-the-head trick did seem to knock some sense into them—or at least into Dad—and they never tried to steal another pie.

Grandma Mathis's daughter, Vivien, owned a bar in Pensacola called the Silver Slipper. She had a pet monkey that she kept at the bar, and his name was King—maybe short for King Kong, or maybe it was named after Elvis. I'm not sure. But Uncle Bill said King was just plain crazy. I think they just plain drove him crazy.

He tells a story of how they made these peashooters out of straws, and they would steal dried beans from the jar in Grandma's kitchen. Again, Jimmy was volunteered to do the dirty work. I guess Grandma didn't get as upset over stolen beans as she did a stolen pie.

They would go down to the Silver Slipper and shoot beans at King through their peashooters and make the monkey even crazier. Kind of like a version of a live-action video game today. Dad and Billy were the Mario Brothers running around and shooting their beans at some specified target. I don't think they were collecting any gold coins or points for prizes. They didn't care. The prize was just having fun. And since real life doesn't have an on-off switch or need batteries, they would play all day. Then go back to Grandma's, go to bed, wake up, and repeat the fun all over again the next day.

Dad would talk about his summers in Pensacola with such vivid animation in his voice and such a fondness for his grandmother and family who lived there. Summers in Florida were special. Time spent with his family and siblings was so precious. Summer at Strawbridge really meant summer in Florida. There were good times and good memories created for the Mathis kids.

Home for the Holidays

Just like in the summertime, the holidays were a time to go home and be with your family, if you had one to go to. Thanksgiving, Christmas, and Easter were the designated holidays that the boys were able to spend with their families. By the time Dad and Billy were able to go back to Bowie the first time, Strawbridge probably felt more like home. But as the holidays approached, it was exciting to think about playing with Richard, Ronnie, Sara, and Inez again. And they would be able to find out about what was going on at their new home in DC and hear about their school and the new friends they had made.

As with many families, Christmas was a special time. Dad and Billy were going home for Christmas, and their brothers and sisters living in DC were coming home, too. Granddaddy would make the long drive out to Strawbridge to pick them up for the winter holiday. He would also go to the Swartzell House and pick up the rest of the family.

Bowie wasn't much, but it was still home. Somehow, their father always tried to make the holidays special. Kids today would probably think it was pretty lame if they only got one gift from Santa. But that one gift was usually the one thing you had been wishing for all year. So when you actually got it, it was extra special.

My uncle Bill tells the story of how, on one rare Christmas, Santa really outdid himself. There was excitement as on any other Christmas. But on this particular Christmas morning when they woke up, there was more than they had thought possible under the tree.

They still don't know how he did it or how he got the presents into the house. When they had come home the day before, they had searched every hiding place possible to see if there was evidence of what Santa was bringing for them that Christmas. They never found anything. They looked everywhere inside and everywhere outside. There were not that many secret places in the Bowie house for gifts to hide. But on Christmas morning, when they tiptoed downstairs, under the tree were four bright and shiny new bicycles for the boys and two beautiful frilly dolls for the girls. There really was a Santa Claus!

Uncle Bill said, thinking back, that he had never seen anything so amazing, and the boys couldn't wait to ride around on their new bikes. But my uncle also realizes now that, given the financial situation of the family at that time, it was more than likely that their father had found scraps of bikes left out for trash by someone else. As they say, "One man's trash is another man's treasure." So I guess Dad got it honest. Granddaddy was very handy and resourceful. Using the skills he learned at the ironworks company, he would have been able to rebuild the bikes and spit shine them so they looked like new. For the Mathis boys, they were brand new. They would now be able to go anywhere on those bikes—ride around the farm or ride to the moon. The bikes and their imaginations were the tickets to new adventures.

Dad would also talk about the tradition of going to get a Christmas tree and decorating it as a family on Christmas Eve. Granddaddy would wait until the family was together to mark the traditions of the season. There were special ornaments that their mother had saved, and they would put them on the tree with care. Each one had a story of where it came from and how it came to be on their tree and part of their Christmas story. The children would make paper garlands and string popcorn and cranberries to hang on the tree.

Then the most fun part was at the end. The children would stand back from the tree, and Granddaddy would give them each a handful of cotton balls. They would throw the cotton balls at the tree. In their minds they were no longer cotton balls. They had become real snowballs. And, when they threw them, wherever they landed on the tree was where they would stick.

Dad would tell Debbie and me about how it didn't snow much in the South where Oliver and Sarah had come from, so this is what they did to make it look like there was snow on the tree. They thought it was great. One Christmas Eve when I was little, we threw cotton balls at our tree, too. Dad was trying to recreate that special moment from his childhood and bring it to life for us. Since Debbie and I knew the difference between real snowballs and cotton balls, it did not have quite the same effect for us. But I could tell that Dad was remembering his Christmases as a boy, and the look in his eye was brighter than the star on top of our tree. Maybe just for tradition's sake, I will share this story with my daughter this coming Christmas. Maybe we can throw cotton balls, too, and think of them as snowballs to honor Dad.

Another Christmas tradition was to always get gifts in your stocking. For Dad's family it was always a special treat every year to get nuts like walnuts and hazelnuts. And they always got an orange. This was an incredible gift as they were not always available in the winter, and they were like a taste of sunshine and a reminder of their family in Florida. It seems silly to think about that today. Most kids would think Santa was crazy if fruit and nuts was all you got in your stocking. But for the Mathis kids, these treats were priceless.

Dad continued this tradition in our house every Christmas. We never forgot what it meant to get something so rare in the winter. While today oranges are readily available and abundant, even in the winter, I wanted to pass on this tradition to my daughter. So, this past Christmas and Christmases in the future, she will get nuts and an orange in her stocking. A reminder of Pop-Pop and that we are blessed to have a taste of summer at any time. I am not sure what made me smile more—imagining her face thinking all she got in her stocking was nuts and an orange or the thought of Dad's face as a little boy, so happy to be getting nuts and an orange in his stocking. Always grateful.

Easter also was a fun time at the Mathis house. When the kids would come home, the girls would dye the eggs, and I guess Granddaddy would hide them. They would take all day to try to find the hidden eggs. They would take breaks to play other games and then eat a big dinner. I used to joke with Dad that maybe they left the eggs out there until summertime on purpose so they would be good and ready and smelling ripe for their train ride to Florida.

Thanksgiving was also a special time. The family would gather together and give thanks for the blessings they had all year. Apparently, with the help of his girls, Granddaddy learned to be a pretty good cook. Dad never talked much about the other holidays. To him, Christmas was always the most special. But Uncle Bill recalls that there was always a turkey for Thanksgiving with all the trimmings. Lots of stuffing, potatoes, corn, and beans. Maybe Grandma Mathis had sent one of her special pies. But at the end of each of these holidays and the time spent catching up and playing with their brothers and sisters, the time together would come to an end.

Then it was back to Strawbridge or Swartzell. Back to their new lives and their new routines. I am sure as the years went by, they got used to the life they were living and that they were living it apart from their family. It became normal for them. You would think as young children they would come to resent that they didn't live life like other families. But that didn't happen. Dad and his family appreciated all that they had and all they had been given. Holidays were a special time with family. Those times together were limited, so they made sure to make the most of them.

More Than an Education

The boys at Strawbridge attended the local schools. Jimmy had been going to school in Bowie. However, probably not on a regular basis after his mother died. When he moved to Sykesville, the school needed to determine his abilities and what grade level he should start. What I know is that despite his age that first year at Strawbridge, he was placed a grade behind at school. Ordinarily, he would have started eighth grade, but they placed him in the seventh grade for the second half of the school year. He had arrived at Strawbridge in December 1950, and after the holiday, he started the Sykesville School in January 1951.

It was quickly determined that he was a pretty smart fellow and handled the academic subjects with ease. So at the end of the school year, he was tested again, and in the fall of 1951, he started ninth grade. They bumped him up one year so he would be with students his own age with the same academic skills. This would prove to be a pretty fateful action.

Apparently, Dad was very likeable and very popular. The caption under his senior year picture said, "Skin—cute and very popular—continuous talker—our class President and a class clown—member of the double quartet—versatile and well-liked." You could say the same things about the man I knew, too. He never changed much as he got older. He was also very smart. He did extremely well in school, and his teachers loved him. Mr. and Mrs. Searle were two of the favorite teachers of the senior class. Mr. Searle wrote in Dad's senior yearbook, "If you handle your future problems as well as you tackled your many tasks this year, you will go far in life. Don't be afraid to tackle the big ones."

Jimmy was the class President starting in ninth grade and remained the President of his class all through high school. He was a natural-born leader. This is how he met the love of his life, Lois. Lois was the last of the Harp girls. There were four Harp sisters—Marilyn, or Molly; Pauline, or Peanie; Beverly; and finally, Lois. Just as Jimmy was a consummate leader,

Lois was the ultimate organizer and kept everyone, including her class, on track. She was the class secretary for all four years of high school.

As class officers, Jimmy and Lois worked together on every activity, every event for their class. I have this picture in my head of the first meeting of the class officers and their meeting for the first time. Dad calls the meeting to order and turns to Mom to read the minutes of the last meeting. Their eyes meet, and there are instant sparks. Not too romantic, but there weren't too many places beyond school to meet people to date. I really don't think it was love at first sight. I think the sparks came much later.

As Mom tells the story, they really became a couple in eleventh grade. Since Dad didn't have a car, they double dated with her best friend, Nancy Kelly, and her boyfriend, Pat Renehan. Pat was from Howard County, and he had a car. The four of them went everywhere together. Though I am not sure where "everywhere" would have been as there were not too many places to go in those days.

By their senior year, it was obvious to all that Jimmy and Lois were a couple. The deal was sealed with the senior play. They both had lead roles in a play called *The Good Egg*. The irony of that title is that Lois's nickname had always been Eggy ever since she was a little girl. The name had started when a man at the little store on the corner of Oakland Mills and Liberty Roads had called her that one time, and it stuck. Dad's nickname was Skin—his brothers called him that since he was so skinny. He had bird legs and little feet. We always joked that we didn't know how his feet held him up. His brother Billy morphed the name *Skin* into *Skinbeezy*. Almost every card he sent, from wherever he was overseas on another tour of duty when he was in the navy, started out the same way—"Heeeeyyyy Skinbeezy!" You could almost hear my uncle shouting it out, jumping right off the postcard, with extra emphasis on the "beezy."

Dad and Mom were leads in the senior play, class officers, members of the school chorus—Double Quartet for Dad and Triple Trio for Mom. They did everything together. There was even a senior trip to New York. Country bumpkins went to the big city. It was so exciting for them.

They went to the B&O Railroad in Baltimore to catch the train to New York City. This trip had to be expensive, so I am sure they worked on fund-raising activities all year so the whole class could go. I think the auxiliary group at Strawbridge would have helped fund the trip for their boys who were seniors. Mr. Bowers, the school principal, and their teachers Mr. and Mrs. Searle, along with some parents, would have chaperoned the trip. Can you imagine taking high-school seniors on an overnight trip today? For several days? I can't imagine anyone allowing it or the security clearances you would need to make it happen. I need child-abuse clearance, background checks, and criminal record checks just to be able to drop something off at my daughter's school today. But in 1955, this trip was certainly a real treat and a highlight for the seniors at Sykesville High School.

They stayed at the Taft Hotel in New York. They visited all the tourist sites of the city—the Statue of Liberty, the Empire State Building, and the United Nations building. They saw the Rockettes at Radio City Music Hall and went to a show on Broadway—Cole Porter's *Can-Can*. According to Mom, this show was pretty risqué for its day, and she is not sure how the school was able to let them see it. But they loved it! They even went to see The Perry Como TV show that was taped in New York.

It was an amazing adventure for the students. And for Dad, it was a long way from Bowie. It was a long way from Sykesville, too, for his classmates. For many of the young boys and girls who got to go, it was their first time in a big city. It was really a big deal and made lasting memories for all of them.

Jimmy and Lois both graduated on June 12, 1955, with honors. Dad had done extremely well in his school career, and my grandfather came to Sykesville for the big event. His firstborn was graduating from high school. This was a big milestone to accomplish, and I wonder if my grandfather realized that the decisions he had made so long ago and the path he had put his children on had led to this moment. The tough choices he had made years before had made this event possible for his son.

**Jimmy and his father, Oliver,
Sykesville High School graduation.
June 12, 1955.**

Dad was offered a full scholarship to the Air Force Academy. He had wanted to fly. Unfortunately, he didn't know it, but he had very bad eyesight and did not pass the eye exams necessary to be able to fly a plane. He thought his dream of flight was over. Not one to stew over the disappointing news, he opted instead to pursue Engineering School at the University of Maryland. If he couldn't fly planes, he was going to build them.

The summer after graduation, Jimmy and Lois continued to see each other. Dad worked odd jobs and maintained his chores at the Strawbridge farm. Mom and her friend Nancy worked at the five and dime in Baltimore. They would take the bus into Baltimore to get to work. For those who do not know, a five and dime was a drugstore or pharmacy. Sometimes it was called a five-and-dime because you could buy items for a nickel or a dime. They were the predecessors of the dollar stores of today. There are even Five Below stores today—it's just the five is now five dollars, not five cents! Inflation in action.

Lois then got a job at the Franklin Balmar Corporation. She worked as a file clerk and did clerical work for a Mr. Strosky. He offered to send her to stenographer school to learn shorthand and typing. She hated it. She could not imagine this would be her life ambition.

She went to the YWCA in Baltimore two nights a week anyway to take the necessary classes. She had to take the bus from Sykesville to get there. She had long days on the days without school and now even longer days with adding night school twice a week. On the days she didn't have school, she rode to work with Mrs. Ruth Conaway and Mr. New. The carpooling got her there safely, and she didn't have to ride the bus on those days.

By the fall of 1955, both Jimmy and Lois were falling into new routines of new schools and work. They were not together every day as they had been at Sykesville High. They didn't like being apart. And so they did something very foolish, very irrational, and very romantic. Maybe a little irresponsible. On November 25, 1955, they got married! They were eighteen.

It was Thanksgiving weekend. As my uncle Richard recalls that particular Thanksgiving, he thought it was odd that only Billy had come home from Strawbridge. All the other Mathis kids were home for the holiday and wondering why Jimmy wasn't there for dinner. Granddaddy would have made the traditional turkey with all the trimmings. When they all sat down for the Thanksgiving feast, Granddaddy told them that Jimmy and Lois had eloped.

As Mom remembered their wedding day, it was very cold. And as she and Dad headed out on their honeymoon weekend to Richmond, Virginia, it started to snow. A light snow, but she still remembers thinking it was a very far drive in a tumbledown car. It was an adventure for sure—both the drive to Richmond and starting a life journey with her Jimmy.

Mom had saved her money from working in Baltimore to buy a beautiful brown faux fur coat that she wore over her wedding dress. Her wedding dress was not traditional. It was beige satin with a floral-type design on it—tea length with three-quarter sleeves. She had bought brown shoes and a matching brown purse to go with the coat. She still has the brown leather purse. A sentimental keepsake.

They didn't have a big church wedding. They didn't have a reception. They didn't have much at all. They didn't have a care in the world. But they had each other. They went to Richmond, Virginia, in Granddaddy's old 1949 Hudson. It was the same rusty car that had brought Dad to Sykesville that fateful day many years before. Now, it was taking him on a different ride. It would end up being a lifetime journey.

Little did they know this was the beginning of what would become more than sixty years of a lifetime together. Because what they lacked in frills and frivolous wedding details, they made up for with love. Lots of love. Seriously. Do you really need napkins and matchbooks with your name on them to show your undying love? Mom and Dad proved you do not.

**Jimmy and Lois on their wedding day,
front porch of the Harp house on Oakland Road,
Sykesville, Maryland. November 25, 1955.**

SECTION 2

The Man

A little nonsense now and then is relished by the wisest men.

—JOSEPH ADDISON

Dad at the C&P Telephone Company office, circa 1973.

The Rocket Scientist

MY FATHER HAD so many facets to him. You could describe him as being kind of like an onion. Peel back the layers, and you would find something new, something about him that would surprise you. He and Lois had gotten married so young and started their life together so fast. Like they were pushing the gas pedal all the way to the floor. As if they had some predetermined deadline to meet. If they did, only they knew it. I am sure many said that their union would never last. They had started too young. But those people didn't know that they were dealing with two people very in love and very motivated to prove everyone wrong. Some would call it being a little hardheaded.

Jimmy got a job with the Glenn L. Martin Company and continued to go to school at night. He was still in pursuit of an engineering degree. Martin's, its short name, was located near Dundalk, Maryland, way on the other side of Baltimore from Sykesville. It is now known as the Lockheed Martin Corporation.

Almost nine months to the day after they were married, my sister Debbie was born. Her full name is Deborah Jane Mathis, but she quickly became Debbie—sometimes just Deb or Debber, as our aunt Beverly used to call her. The middle name Jane was to honor my dad's momma. Dad and Mom lived in an apartment in Pikesville, Maryland, on the second floor of an old house. It had lots of steps. Mom remembers it was very hard to haul groceries and everything you needed for a baby up and down all those steps. Every time you went out the door, you had to haul the baby stuff down the steps, and then when you got back, you had to haul it all back up again.

She also remembered times in the winter when you could put the baby food and milk out on the roof in the snow to keep it cold when you lost power. Apparently, that happened pretty often. Back then, you didn't have the convenience of a generator to kick on when the electricity went out. You just made do with candles and flashlights, or maybe a little snow, until the electricity came back on.

At this time in their lives, another man of the cloth stepped into Dad's path. It always seemed to happen at just the right time. It may have seemed like a small thing at the time, but Reverend Leadbetter from the Baptist church they attended provided Dad with the means to carry out the dream of owning a home and raising a family of his own in it. The reverend introduced them to Betty Myers, who ran a nursery school called Pikesville Nursery and Kindercraft. She was a member of the Methodist church across the street from the Baptist one that Mom and Dad were attending. Mom met Miss Betty (that's what everyone called her), and she went to work at the nursery school. For Lois, this was the beginning of what would become a lifetime of teaching children. It was the late 1950s, and Debbie was now of the age to be able to go to nursery school. Since Mom was working at the school, Debbie was able to attend free of charge.

Miss Betty was more than the woman who ran the school; she became a lifelong friend of our family. She mentored Mom in early-childhood education and supported Mom's love of music. Lois played the piano and sang songs with the children. She still does that today. And there is not a person she has taught who doesn't remember "the Piano Lady" and the songs they learned to commemorate every season and holiday. She instilled a love of music in many children in Pikesville. Eventually, she did that for children in Sykesville, too.

The money that Lois earned at the nursery school was put into a bank account every week. The money was earmarked for a special dream purchase. By 1962, small ranchers—starter homes, really—were being built in Sykesville. Lois's sister Pauline had already moved into her home on Monroe Avenue. The money Mom saved was enough to buy a piece of land on Marvin Avenue—just one street away from her sister. Jimmy and

Lois bought the land and then borrowed money from Sykesville Building and Loan to build their first home. A home of their own. If you just conjured up thoughts of a scene from *It's a Wonderful Life*, you would be right. At that time, Sykesville was a lot like Bedford Falls, the town in the movie.

In early 1963, Jimmy and Lois moved into their new home on Marvin Avenue in Sykesville. Debbie was now six. For years Debbie had been asking for a little sister. She asked at Christmas, for her birthday, every chance she got. April of that same year, Debbie finally got her wish, and I was born. I came into the world at the new maternity ward in Carroll County Hospital in Westminster, Maryland.

Jimmy continued to work at Glenn L. Martin Company. He worked with a man named Warren Bombhardt. He became a mentor for Dad and a very dear friend of the family. Mr. Warren, as Debbie and I called him, lived off Cold Spring Lane near Baltimore. When we went to visit him, it was always such an adventure as we got to go to the city. Thinking back, it was probably much like Mom and Dad when they went to New York on their senior class trip and were seeing a big city for the first time. We thought Mr. Warren lived so far away. Funny that years later, I would do the same commute to that city every day for work.

Mr. Warren traveled all over the world, and he always brought back wonderful souvenirs for us from his trips. Debbie and I didn't care that we didn't get to go to those places. He would tell us stories of his adventures, and we felt like we were there, too. He brought us dolls and musical instruments and toys made of clay. He also gave us books. Lots of books. To this day, we both have a passion for reading. We were inspired at a young age, and he could provide the classics for us to read.

One of my favorite books was *A Child's Garden of Verses* by Robert Louis Stevenson. I would read it incessantly, and my favorite poem in the book was "My Bed Is a Boat." I would literally get on my bed and pretend it was a boat as I read the poem. Sailing everywhere my mind would take me. We didn't need to travel far or need technology to kick-start our imaginations. Mr. Warren brought the world to us through his gifts and books, and we could go to those faraway places anytime. In our minds, anyway.

Dad also worked with another man at Martin's whose name was Lyle Wallis. He was a little bit older than Dad and had worked at Martin's a little longer. It was an exciting time at the company as it had received defense contracts from the government, which meant the company was going to be designing and building planes and warcraft machines. Glenn L. Martin was also awarded contracts through the space program, and certain employees were working on rockets and parts for rockets that would eventually send men to the moon. Dad was one of those lucky employees chosen to work on the space missions.

Prior to the Apollo missions that would put man on the moon for the first time in 1969, there were the Gemini missions. The Gemini missions were part of NASA's second human spaceflight program. These missions' programs started in 1961 and ended in 1966. Jim Mathis just happened to be at the right place at the right time. It didn't hurt that he was scary smart. Dad may not have been able to fly planes, but he was now going to get to work on rockets that would enable men to go to the moon. I think he was probably "over the moon" to get to do this and work on these special projects.

I had always heard about his work at Martin's and that he had worked on rockets. However, I didn't know the half of it. It was not until recently when we were going through so many papers after Dad passed away that we discovered how important his work was to the space mission. On May 4, 1965, Dad received a Certificate of Creative Scientific Achievement from the Martin Company, the aerospace division of

Martin Marietta Corporation. On this same date, he and Lyle Wallis were also served with a patent issued by the United States Patent Office. They had developed a process for resistance welding through a butyl rubber weld-through sealant. What the heck was that? Yeah, that's what I asked, too. And who would have thought to make it in the first place? But this was a breakthrough for the program. And, apparently, it was pretty important.

This special sealant was resistant to high temperatures and pressure that would become necessary for the rockets headed to the moon. It would keep the air pressure inside the rocket safe for the astronauts and keep the elements in space during the flight from entering the rocket. Dad really was a rocket scientist. The first mission that used this special welding process was the Gemini-Titan No. 3. The astronauts on that mission were Virgil I. Grissom and John W. Young. I am sure they appreciated that special welding. They may not have known it was there, but I am sure they were thankful for men like Dad, who were making their space travel possible and safer.

This was a really cool time for our country and for all involved in the space program. To most people who know my father, this little factoid about him may come as a surprise. Dad was not the type to go around talking about his work or telling stories about what he did at work every day. He just went to work, collected his paycheck every week, and put his money in the bank to support his family. If Dad made a dollar, he saved at least eighty cents.

Secretly, inside, I am sure he loved to go to work and was excited to get to do what he loved. He really was a science geek, a bit of a nerd. And when I got to high school and needed to take subjects like physics and calculus, I was very thankful for his nerdiness. There were many nights spent at our kitchen table trying to solve never-ending equations that seemed to be written in Greek. At least, to me. But Dad understood

Greek and math and science. He got it, and he patiently explained it to me until I got it, too.

Dad continued to work at the Glenn L. Martin Company until 1967. That year, Martin's lost its space contracts. North American Aviation Corporation was awarded the design and production contracts by NASA going forward. And therefore, many employees at Martin's lost their jobs. Including Dad. He now had a wife, two children, and a mortgage. Fortunately for us, he was not out of work for long.

The theme of good things happening for him through the church or connections to the church continued. There was a man who lived across the street from the church they attended, and he gave Dad information about a possible job lead. It was with the C&P Telephone Company. This random acquaintance through the church, Harry Andrews, put a new, exciting opportunity in Dad's career path. Harry knew the phone company had jobs for which they were hiring new people, and he shared this news with Dad. So Dad contacted C&P, got the job, and became a C&P Telephone man.

While Dad was doing amazing things at work and continued to work hard at his new job with the phone company, he also continued to get his education. Education and his thirst for knowledge were things he pursued his whole life. He had continued his secondary education at community colleges, and in 1968 he finally received his associate's degree from Catonsville Community College. Oliver was there for the big event. I was, too. I was only five at the time and do not really remember it. But it was a big deal and another milestone for Jimmy. And he didn't stop there. He kept on going—learning more, doing more, collecting more degrees.

Wichita Lineman

Dad joined the C&P Telephone Company in 1967. It's funny that he worked at the phone company and we always called him "the phone man," but I don't think any of his jobs ever really involved working with an actual telephone. As you drove down the road, you would see men climbing the telephone poles and fixing wires. Dad didn't do any of those jobs, either.

Dad spent most of his career at the phone company. He was there when it was C&P. And he was still there later when it became Bell Atlantic. Later still, it was taken over by Verizon. In the beginning, he worked in the engineering department. At first he was in the Baltimore office, and in later years, he would make the commute to the office in Arlington, Virginia. I personally don't know how he stood the long drives. I've had to do it, too, and it's no picnic. Maybe it was the carpool buddies that made the unending time in the car less painful. Believe it or not, Sykesville was becoming a commuter town for jobs in Baltimore and Washington, DC. Folks like Dad spent the better part of three hours a day in the car to get to and from these jobs.

However, as I think back to that time, I don't remember Dad ever missing a family dinner. That was a sacred time of the day. And he was always present for after-school activities, too—games, concerts, and 4-H events. I always remember him being there to cheer us on and to support whatever our passion was at the time.

When I think about my 4-H days (and there were many!), Mom and Dad were always there, side by side. Every public-speaking competition, every demonstration day, every fashion show, every county fair and state fair, too. The Carroll County 4-H Fair was always the first week of August, and the Maryland State Fair in Timonium, Maryland, was the last week of August. We were at both fairs every summer to enter our projects and collect our ribbons, and Dad is part of every one of those memories. As a working parent now, I don't know how he did it. When did he have time to go to work?

Our dinner conversations during the phone years were peppered with references to the Ma Bell companies and Baby Bells as Dad talked about his day at work. I am not really sure what it all meant. It just all sounded important, and Dad must have been doing a great job as he was promoted several times over the years and took on more responsibility each time. At one point he was part of the organizational design team and development staff. He led a committee with representatives from all departments, who were responsible for looking for ways to improve processes and products and make the departments more efficient. The end result would be less expense to the company and more profit.

He also spoke one time about having to testify at hearings on what were affectionately called "the rate wars." I didn't know what that meant at the time but would picture him in something like *Mr. Smith Goes to Washington*, and he would have to go before a jury or something. Sounded so important and must have been stressful as during that time he would always bite his lip. We first noticed it at dinner one night. He looked like he had grown a red mustache. He had bitten his upper lip so much that it was red for days. It's funny that my daughter now does the same thing when something is weighing on her mind or making her anxious. My niece used to do it, too. We called it "Pop-Pop face."

The rate wars were really about rate relief for certain segments of the public and businesses using the telephone services. Dad represented C&P Telephone Company, and he and public attendees would go before the public-service commission to present data on whether services warranted a rate increase. Each state had its own commission, so the hearings that took place were very time consuming, and the results were different from state to state. Dad would travel to each location to present the data on behalf of the company. The job was to create more revenue for C&P. Pretty important stuff. And Dad was at the heart of it.

His last post with the company was a regional position in the real-estate group for Bell Atlantic managing five states. He was still not working with actual telephones. Back then, there was not a work-from-home option. Employees did not have the luxury of computers at their homes, and there were not yet mobile devices to work from anywhere. So no actual work was done outside the office. It allowed employees to enjoy the time at home with their families in the evenings and on the weekends. I actually think this was a good thing. Family came first, work second. I know it always did for Dad.

At some point, Dad actually got to bring home a new piece of equipment that was in development that the employees were getting to test. It was a portable phone that you carried in a bag on your shoulder. We called it a bag phone. We thought it was the coolest thing. It allowed you to take your phone outside or anywhere, although I think Debbie and I had already tried to take the green phone that hung on the wall in our kitchen outside anyway. Our infamous green phone had a long cord made even longer as we had stretched it out to the patio or down the hallway to our bedrooms to get more privacy. That green phone is still hanging on the wall in Mom's kitchen today. And it still works. Dad refused to ever get rid of it. Why? Because, like I said, it still worked.

The cord was a tangled mess from overstretching it, but you could still make a phone call. I am surprised he wasn't still using a rotary phone. For those of you reading this who may not know what that is, ask someone over fifty years of age who can tell you. They will recall that it took about three minutes just to dial a phone number, and you had to know the number or look it up in a telephone book that was at least three inches thick. If you dialed the wrong number, you had to start all over again from the beginning. With today's smart phones, you can call ten phone numbers, leave three messages, look up the menu at your favorite restaurant, and book a reservation all in the time it took to make one call on a rotary phone.

But back to the cool bag phone. Up to that point, we just thought push-button phones were cool. The bag phone was literally in a bag like a tote bag that you carried on your shoulder. It was a far cry from the mobile phones today, but they had to start somewhere. Believe it or not, the mobile bag telephone was cutting-edge technology. We used to joke with Dad that he was like that guy from the show *Get Smart*—what was next, the shoe phone?

While at the phone company, Dad continued to pursue his education. The company had a tuition reimbursement program as one of the perks for their employees. Dad took advantage of this benefit and was accepted into the Johns Hopkins University engineering school. He would work all day, and then two or three nights a week, depending on the semester and class load, he went to night school.

Some of the guys he worked with at the phone company went to Hopkins at night, too. There was a group of them who would meet before classes started to grab some dinner. Dad had been taught at a young age that saving your pennies mattered. He took his lunch to work every day, and on the days he had night school, Mom would pack two sandwiches—one for lunch and one for dinner. Dad would save the paper bag she put them in and the wax paper the sandwiches were wrapped in, too. Everything was used over and over again until it was completely used up. Never any waste. Lessons learned at Strawbridge.

He would meet the guys on campus so they could all eat something together before class. Some nights, they had two classes. So around 8:00 p.m., between classes, the group would meet again to get coffee and get energized to get through the rest of the night. Johns Hopkins was about a forty-five-minute drive from Sykesville, so night school days were very long days.

The group of guys had clicked working at the phone company first, and then the friendship expanded while they were going to night school together. They had come from different professional backgrounds— Bethlehem Steel, Bell Labs, Western Electric, B&O Railroad, and Dad from Martin Marietta. Dad was used to diversity from his Strawbridge days. The forty brothers he had there were from all walks of life and be- came his family. This work family was a bit like that—a blended family of work experience. We only knew them by their last names. Dad always referred to them as Walton, Geldy, Mosner, and Jollett.

They were a new generation of employees hired to bring forth new technologies to the communication industry. This group was thought of as the "outsiders." The employees already there had come up through the ranks of the telephone service company. The outsiders bonded at work, forged a deeper bond at school, and decided to take it a step fur- ther by creating a poker night so they could have some fun, too.

The "boys" settled on a group of seven. Lucky seven? Maybe. The card group would rotate from house to house, with each person host- ing once a month. They played nickel and dime games. No one ever lost more than ten bucks, and no one ever won more than ten or twenty bucks. It was all for fun—playing the card games, sharing stories of work and school, and creating friendships that would last a lifetime.

One of the guys shared with me that when they first started to play on Friday nights, they each used to bring a case of their favorite beer, and they smoked cigars and shared stories about women. (Their wives, I'm sure!) By the time they were reaching the age of retirement from the company, the poker group had been playing cards for more than twenty years. Now when the group got together, it was a case of Diet Coke, no smoking of any kind, and they swapped stories about their doctors and what meds they were taking to keep their joints moving and life going. The vices were different, but the friendship remained.

Another poker group buddy shared that Dad was known for never getting caught at bluffing on the cards in his hand. If he was betting, you knew he had the goods, and you better fold your hand. Dad was never much of a gambler. He bought the occasional lottery ticket. So in poker, he would never risk a bluff. He was always honest. Even at cards.

I know that Mom still has the green wool blanket the guys used when it was Dad's turn to host the poker game at our house. The blanket covered the poker table. It kind of looked like the green felt on the game tables you see at casinos. When we were cleaning out stuff in the basement at Mom's house, we came across the green blanket in a pile of other old blankets. The old quilt blanket we used to use for picnics, the one for the beach. And Dad's old poker blanket. Funny how knowing it's still around and Dad is not makes me sad somehow. Nostalgic. It makes me sad thinking of them sharing their war stories over a game of cards. The battles they shared at work and at school. Mom and I just stood there and cried. It's weird the things that will strike you and stir up memories and emotions.

The Hopkins crew also worked on school projects together. They would sometimes meet at the library to study or to do their research for projects. At that time the information and knowledge you needed was not at your fingertips on a laptop or mobile device. You had to go to your local library or the school library to use the books and reference materials to find what you needed.

While Dad would have gone to the school library to get access to certain books, periodicals, and reference materials, he also could have used our home set of the World Book Encyclopedia series. We had the whole set! Mom and Dad had bought the set one book at a time. The topics were organized by letter, and each letter had its own book. We would get one letter at a time. Then updates were provided each year. They sat on a bookshelf in my bedroom. I guess when I first used them for book reports for school, the topics had to be things like anteaters or Brazil. We didn't have the *Z* book yet, so we couldn't do a report on zebras. We had to wait a while for that book to come. I don't remember if you paid monthly and received a new book each month or you paid as you could afford. Either way, it was a two-year wait to get to read and write about zebras!

Mom and Dad had bought the set from Mom's cousin, who was selling encyclopedias to make extra money. For us, whenever we had to do any report or project for school (and that included Dad, too) the books were like our hard drive, our brains were the computer, and our fingers were the mouse actively searching for information to write about our subjects and topics and back up our notes.

Dad also owned almost every copy of *Life* magazine and *National Geographic* magazine. It was almost like our own set of periodicals you would find at the library. This was another way he exposed Debbie and me to everything going on around the world—through written word, stories, and pictures we would see in the magazines. We learned about African tribes, space missions, Mars, adventures to the North Pole and the South Pole, too. Like the books from Mr. Warren, these magazines shared knowledge about things we would never find in Sykesville.

Dad and his Hopkins classmates had to do several engineering projects to obtain their degrees. One in particular turned out to be quite an engineering marvel. Dad and the group had to complete a final project to graduate. Dad had already worked on rockets and received a patent for his unique discoveries. This project, needed for graduation, would prove to be no different. It was way ahead of its time.

It was the final semester of 1975. The group's final project was to create something for their advanced mechanical engineering class. At this point in time, the auto industry was doing everything it could to keep up with demand, as more and more families owned a car, and sometimes they owned two. There were also many more cars on the road as people commuted farther to work. This meant there were more accidents. By 1973, front passenger-side airbags had started to become standard in some cars. Dad and his team decided they were going to try to create a driver-side airbag. And they did!

Apparently, it was such a novel thing that they, of course, passed their class with flying colors. Their professor realized the project was something pretty extraordinary and entered the project into an auto industry invention contest taking place in Chicago. We never knew about that. Dad never mentioned it. It turns out they won second place. I now wonder, what won first? Who beat them? We will never know.

As we cleaned out closets and the garage after Dad passed away, we found interesting mementos of Dad's life and the strange things he thought were important enough to save. Lots of tools, tickets, and brochures from places visited on family trips. Small things, big things, sometimes odd things, and no understanding of what the things meant to him. A lifetime of collecting things and never letting anything go. But tucked away in a square box in the garage were the written documents and the sample of the airbag they had created for the Hopkins project. I think my brother-in-law found it as he and Debbie were helping clean out the garage. The garage was full of Dad's treasures—we called it junk. But sometimes when you're not really looking, you find an actual treasure. The document was a very thick, hand-typed report with hand-drawn schematics of their airbag design. The box also had a strange-looking pink fabric thing.

My sister, also a 4-H'er, had actually sewn the airbag sample together using our household Singer sewing machine. I find it funny that the fabric was pink. I picture in my mind these four grown men giving their formal presentation with their precisely engineered, scientific drawings. It had to be right in order for them to graduate. Everything had to be just so. They had to walk through all the design work and rationale and show how the airbag would deploy in an actual accident and work to save lives. When the time came to pull out the sample and show how it worked, it was made of pink satin! Probably some remnant left from a 4-H project. Dad would have thought it would be extravagant to buy additional fabric if you had enough on hand. I can hear him now asking, "Who cares what color it is?"

Dad had to have known this project was something pretty special, something worth saving. It had been saved for a long time and put in a safe place. It was really cool it was found. Fitting that Debbie has it now. Probably in the same box and now in a safe place in her garage. She was especially proud to have been a part of the project team. She had made the actual balloon-like airbag.

I am not sure whatever happened to the Hopkins professor or the invention contest entrants and winners. However, it was in the early 1970s that Ford and General Motors were offering cars equipped with airbags. However, due to lack of consumer interest, they were discontinued in the 1977 models. It was with the release of the 1988 models that Chrysler made the passenger-side airbag a standard option. By the early 1990s, airbags were made standard and became widespread in American-made cars for both the passenger and the driver side. Dad and the team had created their airbag in 1975. Genius? Revolutionary? Who knows? Maybe. But it was enough for them to graduate.

Graduation was in June of 1975. I was there. I was twelve, and I re-member being so proud when they called Dad's name. His father, Oliver, was not there for this milestone. He had passed away a few years before, but I know he would have been so proud. I wonder if Dad could hear him yelling from the heavens, "Way to go, Jimmy." He was known to give shout-outs to his boys. And when Dad walked across that stage to get his engineering degree from Johns Hopkins University (with honors, no doubt), a shout-out was definitely deserved.

I think about what was going on in my life when I was twelve compared to Dad's life when he was that same age. His family had faced tragedy and hardships. He was definitely putting things in place so that my life at twelve years old would be different. He was changing the course of our lives, and he was making sure we would not have similar hardships. It just shows you that with goals, determination, and ambition, you can change the direction of a family path in just one generation. Dad made sure our lives would be different. In his mind he was working hard to make our lives better.

Dad ended up working for the phone company until 1994. He was forced into retirement in one of many mergers and downsizings. He was only fifty-seven, but he had put in more than twenty-five years of service to the company. He had worked long and hard. He took his severance and retirement package and moved on to the next post. He knew he wasn't done yet. The next chapter would keep him local. He was offered the opportunity to be the new director of the Carroll County Transit System.

The CTS, as it was known, was a local transit system of about twenty or thirty small buses and vans. They were used to transport people around the county who needed a ride to doctor's offices, hospitals for tests, or shopping for whatever they needed. The ridership was made up of mostly seniors, those who had disabilities or special needs, and those who could not drive themselves. It was a great service that provided independence for many Carroll County residents. With Dad at the helm and his penchant for helping others, it was definitely right up his alley.

He worked there for a number of years, from 1994 to 2000. Under his leadership the number of vehicles and the number of riders increased dramatically. He applied for and received grants from the state and county to subsidize the growing need in the county. We used to joke that he was just making sure people got to Walmart to shop, but he was doing much more than that. CTS was providing an invaluable service to county residents. Dad was making sure that they got where they needed to go and they got there safely.

During Dad's time working for CTS and his continued volunteer work to help others, the good work that he was doing did not go unrecognized. The local TV station, WJZ Channel 13, honored him. He was nominated and chosen as one of thirteen local heroes. Dad was not about the recognition, but we knew he deserved it for all that he did to make sure others got what they needed. We already knew he really was a small-town hero, and it was so great to know that others saw him that way, too.

Prior to leaving Carroll County Transit, the Carroll County commissioners also felt that Dad deserved recognition for his tireless efforts to support seniors and help those who were not able to help themselves. July 21, 2000, was declared Jim Mathis Day in the county. It was just another honor for Dad, one of many for just doing what came naturally for him. We were so proud, and he was so humbled. It's kind of strange that fifteen years later, on the very same day, his days as an angel on this Earth ended.

He retired for good in 2000 at age sixty-three. The days of being paid for employment were done, but his work was not. He would now have 100 percent of his time to devote to his volunteer efforts at the Board of Child Care, church, the Telephone Pioneers and others. The Telephone Pioneers were a group of retired telephone-company personnel. They organized fund-raising efforts to aid the Dove House (a hospice care center in Carroll County) and to help other local family charities in need. Of course, Dad would want to be active in an organization with helping others as its primary mission.

Although Dad had other jobs throughout his life, given the length of time he spent at the telephone company, he would forever be remembered as the Phone Man. There is a song by Glen Campbell called "Wichita Lineman." It's funny now that Dad is gone, whenever that song comes on, it is somehow a reminder of the phone man I lost. Whenever I hear it, the tears are always just below the surface, and I cry. And the song always seems to come on as I drive to Sykesville, just as I cross the bridge over Liberty Dam on Route 26. That's the moment I enter Carroll County. Another sign? I think so.

You probably wonder how I hear this song since it was recorded back in 1968 and is not played much on the radio anymore. Believe it or not, I have it downloaded in my iTunes library, and it's included in a playlist. The soundtrack of my life is very eclectic. In my music library you will find everything from Carole King to Metallica, John Tesh to Van Halen, Brad Paisley to Bon Jovi. And, yes, even Glen Campbell. And when that song randomly comes on, I believe that it's another sign. Dad is tuning into my life and pops up through this song every once in a while. Weird that it always seems to be when I am thinking of him or feeling like I need to talk to him.

Jimmy Webb, who wrote the song (ironic that his name is Jimmy, too), was quoted once saying that the song is actually about a telephone lineman who works really hard, who is forever devoted to his job, and never takes a vacation. It's a simple song about an ordinary man thinking extraordinary thoughts. That was my dad. I guess that is why when I hear the lyrics, it makes me think of him and miss him even more.

Church, Community, and Character

As Dad was working his way up the ranks at the telephone company and working hard on his college degree, he was also devoted to his church and community. I can't remember a time when Dad wasn't doing something for the church. With the church, to the church, something for someone at the church, taking something to the church, picking up something from the church, digging dirt at the church, cleaning up something at the church, going to a meeting at the church. Or he was doing stuff for other people. I think you get the idea. He was doing something all the time. Once he retired, he had time to do more stuff.

Once Mom and Dad fully retired, I can remember talking to them on the phone during the week and asking about their plans for the upcoming weekend. Their to-do list was like a to-do list on steroids. Most people might have a list like theirs to accomplish in a month. They were going to check everything off the list over the weekend. It made me tired just talking about it. My sister and I laugh because we always have a running to-do list. Never seems to end. Cross off two things; add five more things to do. Overachievers Anonymous. The first step is awareness. At least we get it honestly.

That was Dad. And Mom, too. They volunteered for everything. *No* was not in their vocabulary. Well, maybe for Debbie and me when we wanted something like more allowance every week. The answer to our request for more was always more chores so we could work for it and earn it. I'm sure I hated that answer back then, but I'm grateful now to know what it means to work for something, to value its worth. And faith in knowing that hard work will actually take you where you want to go. I'm sure my daughter does not appreciate these lessons at all, but I smile, knowing someday she will, just like me.

As you have read so far, you should realize that church was a constant in Dad's life—in our lives. It didn't matter if it was the Baptist church or the

Methodist one, Dad was just always involved. As a young boy, he was introduced to church. Back then, it was the Baptist church. His early Sunday school teachings provided him with a Christian foundation that he would carry with him throughout his whole life. He could quote Bible scriptures, and he knew all the characters in each of the Bible stories. He understood the lessons that were being taught, but he didn't push his faith on you. I think for Dad it was more a sense of duty, a sense of what was expected of him, rather than a sense of religion. He wasn't someone I would call overly religious or fanatical; it was just a given that every Sunday morning, you would find Dad sitting in a church pew, or sitting with the choir, and Mom would be sitting at the organ. He just lived his life in a Christian way. He didn't know any different.

When he went to live at the Strawbridge Home for Boys, his church way of life continued. The Strawbridge Boys attended St. Paul's Methodist Church. Then when Jim and Lois were first married and lived in Pikesville, they attended the Baptist church again. But when they bought their home and settled back in Sykesville, it was back to Methodist. Makes you think maybe it's not your actual religion that matters. Just that you have faith.

Once they moved back and were living on Marvin Avenue, they regularly attended Oakland United Methodist Church. This church had been Lois's family church for many years, for several generations. It was this back-and-forth that I guess caused some confusion for a time in their lives. Because when I was born, they were not really sure what they were. Baptist or Methodist? And as a result, I was not baptized at birth. It wasn't until I was going through the process of getting confirmed in the church that I had to get baptized first. It was actually kind of a neat thing, since I took the classes and took the baptismal vows for myself.

As a baby you never know what you're going to believe as you get older. I'm still not sure if I believe in all of it, but I consider myself to be a spiritual person. I believe there is a higher power at work, and I believe in signs. So it was at this point in my life, at age twelve, that I was baptized and confirmed on the same day. I had only known the Methodist church—specifically, Oakland United Methodist Church—and I believed all that I had been taught in my Sunday school and confirmation classes. Despite the confusion about which religious doctrine we were going to follow when I was born, by the time I was baptized and confirmed, we were definitely going the Methodist route.

Dad realized as a young man that he had been afforded an opportunity to live a good life and that he had many mentors who had helped him along the way. He was now in a position to become a mentor, too. Just as there had been people put in his path to help him and his family when he lost his mother, he sought out ways to do the same for others. The church was an obvious place to start.

Jim and Lois were not just casual Sunday church service attendees. They were not just Christmas Christians, either. Sorry to say that today, I think that's what I am. I can only seem to get there on holidays. But Mom and Dad went to church every Sunday. Mom still does. They were involved. Jumped in with both feet. There were committees to join and to lead. There were events to plan and social gatherings to attend. The church was a way of life. It was their social scene and their way of making a strong commitment and contributions to the community.

Throughout his years, Dad was a member of the various groups and committees at the church. He was a member of the United Methodist men's group. He was also on the cemetery trustees committee and eventually was the leader of that group. He took a lot of pride in making sure that the families and loved ones of the deceased were treated with compassion and respect.

There was an order and purpose to making sure the deceased were also treated the same. I can't help but think that he would think of his own family and the tragic situation he went through as a young boy. He had learned about the loss of a loved one at an early age. The church had treated his family with compassion and grace. While it had been a difficult time, it had grounded him. For him this was a small way to pay back a debt he felt he owed.

The cemetery trustees were a group in which he could help people through their own difficult times. He could help them with one thing on the list of to-dos when you are planning a funeral for a loved one. As head of the trustees, Dad was also sometimes called upon to help people as they researched family history. Cemetery markers give families information about dates of birth, dates of death, and who was married to whom. He helped with some of these family genealogy projects and enabled people to find out where they came from. He knew from experience it was so important.

He was also on the finance committee and for many Sundays, for many years, stayed after church to count the offering-plate collections. The committee made sure the church stayed afloat financially and that the doors remained open and the lights stayed on. There were also fundraising events to collect additional monies when needed. The church used to host these oyster and ham suppers. I can remember the smell of oysters frying in the oil vats. The men would hand pat them, fry them up, and then serve them to hundreds of hungry Carroll County people who came for miles to eat them. For me, this was not a very good memory.

I realize it was a good thing for the church to make money at a fundraiser, but even today, the smell of oysters makes my stomach roll over. It's that weird black thing in the middle of the oyster when you cut into them to eat them. I used to cover them up with lots of ketchup so I didn't have to see what I was eating. Maybe I should have tried applesauce. Maybe that is why many folks just eat oysters whole. Then you don't have to see what's inside. It took many oysters, literally, to keep the church running.

Dad worked on the finance committee for many years at the church, and eventually, he was treasurer of the church. This was a prominent, important position in the congregation. He worked with the pastor and the various committees to make sure that the financial health of the church was in good standing. He also continued to be a member of several committees within the church, always helping and sometimes leading the way.

The most fitting place that Dad started his involvement with the church and probably the beginning of his self-determined goal to give back to others was with the MYF. Those not associated with the Methodist church may not be familiar with this acronym. You could probably come up with a few choice ideas based on today's lingo and the minimization of the English language into three letters and sound bites. But in the context of the Methodist church, this stands for the Methodist Youth Fellowship.

Dad was the leader of the MYF group at Oakland Church for many years. The funny thing, as I think back on it now, is that he was probably not much older than the youth he was mentoring. Remember, he and Mom had married at age eighteen, and Debbie came along when they were just nineteen. So at the point Dad was working with the MYF group, he was probably in his late twenties or early thirties. And maybe that is why he was able to relate to them in a way that the other elders of the church or their own parents could not.

The teenagers and tweens who were part of this group would meet every week. They formed a small community where they shared their faith, had a safe place to question it, usually did some community service activity, and had fun all at the same time. I was little when Dad was head of this group, so I don't really remember much about it. He was a mentor and leader to many of the church members' children. He had learned the nurturing skills well from the likes of Miss Seymour and Mr. Horn at Strawbridge. There were also kids of those families who lived in and around the community who were allowed to join, too. Back then, there was not much for kids to do after school, on the weekends, or in the summer. They were not overscheduled with different activities every day like kids are today. The MYF was provided a safe place to hang out and gave them something productive to do.

In the late 1960s and early 1970s, there were revolutions and chaos going on around the country. The American youth were questioning the direction of the country's leaders. Sounds a bit like today. It's 2018, and not much has changed. They were being drafted to fight wars they did not believe in. At this point in our history, President John F. Kennedy had been assassinated in 1963. In 1968, his brother Bobby and Martin Luther King were also killed. The Vietnam War was raging on. The headlines on the news included sit-ins, burning bras, drug use, and protests on college campuses. Even for those growing up in the small community of Sykesville, there was a lot to be anxious about with everything that was going on around them. The youth at MYF were looking for someone to guide them, support them, and listen to them. That someone was my father.

To write Dad's story, I needed to reach out to some of the members of the MYF. Those I spoke to said the best quality about Dad was that he was so approachable, easy to talk to. He offered help to them in a nonthreatening way. They felt as though he was only half a generation removed from the things they were dealing with—not a full generation like their parents. Dad—Mr. Mathis or Mr. Jim to them—had also been through a lot already in his short life.

Many of the youth he was working with had not been outside the borders of Carroll County. Some had never been to a big city. While it may seem a bit of a stretch, my father came across to them as worldly. He had traveled to cities. Had been born outside the county. He had traveled by train to Florida every summer with his siblings. He had a good job and was pursuing a college degree. This was not the case for some of the parents of these children. This did not make Dad any better but just gave the appearance of more experience, more exposure to things they might have been dealing with.

He would discuss tough issues with the youth over a game of volleyball. As a team they would work together to solve whatever problems came their way. They learned that they were not alone and that they could accomplish more as a group than just one person. They learned to compromise and negotiate and honed communication skills they would carry with them for life.

They remembered Dad with such high regard and were so saddened by his loss. He had been a strong force in their formative years. Those who knew him as their MYF leader described him with words like *giving, kind, humble, smart, respectful, a good listener.* He listened without judgment and gave them the room they needed to work out their troubles.

One of the MYF boys mentioned that one time, Dad took all the boys outside to help clean one of their cars. It was a red Mustang. A beauty, I was told. A classic. They all got together to help wash it, then clean the inside and wax the outside. Again, this was an activity they were excited to engage in, and at the same time, they could talk about whatever was on their minds, accomplishing something together and working out their issues.

Dad would weigh in with his opinions, and a group consensus could be reached on how to solve whatever was going on. It was a way to get the boys to talk. Sometimes you just have to get stuff off your chest. I am sure that Dad learned these lessons of interaction and communication at Strawbridge. Don't forget, he was raised with forty boys. To maintain order and keep a conflict-free zone at all times at the home, I am certain talking things out was done on a daily basis at Strawbridge. Probably several times a day.

In my conversations with the former MYF members, a story about Dad surfaced, and I feel it truly illustrates the influence he had in his ability to guide others. The details are fuzzy, and that is mostly because my father never shared this story with us. Not even with Mom. He never broke a confidence, and the youth trusted him. But someone was witness to his ability to heal the conflict that was hurting a family at the church.

There was a young girl in the youth group who was struggling with an unknown issue that was tearing her family apart. One particular Sunday, the youth met at the church hall for Sunday school class. The church fellowship hall is about a fifteen-minute walk from the sanctuary where church services were held. In addition to leading the youth group, Dad also taught Sunday school classes. Whatever was going on with this girl and her family, it was apparently something the young girl had confided in Dad, and she was looking for answers, for guidance.

When Sunday school was over, the class walked as a group up Oakland Mills Road to the church for services. Dad and this young girl walked together, lagging behind the rest of the group. The young boy who witnessed this never knew what was troubling the family or what words of wisdom my father shared that day. All he knows is that she obviously took Dad's advice, and it worked. The family was repaired and restored. The young girl was able to work through the friction with her family based on my father's intervention that day.

This is just one example of his strength and goodness. It's signature Jim Mathis. Dad's humble nature would never allow him to discuss what he was doing as he worked with others and helped others. For him, it was just the normal course of business. He expected this of himself and expected it of others. His expectations were very high. He didn't have to advertise what he was doing, whom he was helping, or the success he had in doing it. The people he helped knew, and that was all that mattered.

One such man was in the MYF group as a boy, and he shared with me that Dad had decided to teach him the game of golf. Dad had been taught the game when he went to work at the phone company. Some of the men he worked with would play on Saturdays to work out their frustrations from the week at work. It was also a way to get to know your coworkers better outside the office. Dad played as a way to relax, channel his energy into something else for a period of time (usually four hours), and just to clear his head. Dad always said it was good therapy to chase a little white ball around.

This particular man credits my father with helping him cope with a difficult period in his life. He wasn't sure what direction his life was going to take. He believes that Dad stepped in at just the right time and that golf provided him with the distraction needed to keep him on a straight and narrow path. Taking a confused teenager and teaching him to focus.

Sometimes he and Dad would just hit buckets of balls in the field near our house. Today, that field is full of townhomes and shopping centers. But back in the 1970s, there was lots of green space to hit a golf ball with no fear of hitting anything else for miles. They would grab a bucket of balls on a Saturday afternoon and hit them for hours.

At the same time, he and Dad would share views on religion, education, and politics. Dad never pushed his views; he allowed you to reach your own conclusions. He would use golf analogies to explain life lessons. Always something about working hard and that practice makes perfect to improve and reach your goals.

One time, they actually played a full round of golf at the course at the former Western Maryland College, now McDaniel College in Westminster, Maryland. This young boy, now a man, still plays golf today. He said it's a good way to clear his head or work through something that's giving him a challenge. He remembered Dad as always being comfortable in his own skin, and he always had a twinkle in his eye. Like he had some secret to share, like he had the answer to a riddle or knew the punch line of the joke before anyone else. Dad's sense of humor is something everyone who knew him remember the most and something that they miss. He could always make you laugh, even if it was at yourself.

To this young man, the measure of a man is in his convictions, his faith. In his eyes, at least, Dad certainly measured up. He appreciated that Dad didn't impose his beliefs or ideas. If you were interested in a certain topic and wanted to learn more, then Dad would take you along the way. It didn't matter if it was religion, golf, or something else. He opened up new experiences for the youth to appreciate, gave them new perspectives to ponder. If he didn't know what to offer to educate or encourage them using something from his own experience, then he would lend them a book to read so they could gain their own insights and find their own answers. This particular young man had asked about golf because he knew Dad played the game. So Dad gave him a book about it, told him to learn the rules, gave him old clubs to practice with, and then taught him how to play.

Dad was always learning and searching. I think he felt strongly that a way to work with the youth of MYF was to guide them and help them learn for themselves. Give them a foundation to make up their own minds; let them come up with their own ideas. Sometimes it's just providing the right environment for the learning to happen. At Strawbridge, Dad was given that environment, and he wanted the youth he was mentoring to have the same.

In addition to Dad's church activities, he was also part of other community organizations. I mentioned the Telephone Pioneers, but he was also very active in the local chapter of the Jaycees—the Freedom Jaycees. The *JC* stood for junior chamber, which was a civic organization for young men. Dad was part of this group when he was a young family man and he and Mom had settled back in Sykesville in the 1960s.

The Jaycee members were able to take part in leadership training and provided community service through organized projects. I always remember Dad running off to meetings, events, or something. He never let any grass grow under his feet and rarely sat idle. There was always some mission to be served, someone who needed something, something that needed to be done. Those who knew him or worked with him in any way knew that if you needed something done, done well, and done right, call Jim Mathis. Locally, his reputation always preceded him. People knew Jimmy Mathis. He was like the unelected Mr. Sykesville. People he came in contact with outside Carroll County quickly learned that Jim Mathis was someone who lived life with strong conviction and always put others first.

Almost Full Circle

James O. Mathis was about to make a really big difference. He was getting ready to take on a whole new level of helping others. He would be giving back to those who had helped him and his family so long ago. I am not sure if anyone was paying attention. Especially me.

I was busy with my life. I had been offered an opportunity and a promotion with my job, and I was moving to Charlotte, North Carolina. I didn't realize that greatness was in the making. Dad's lifelong endeavors to help and serve others, at least up to that point in his life, were about to take a giant leap. I am sure for him it was just like any other day. He would have woken up early, made the coffee, and gone to the paper box to get the local paper, and he would be reading said paper by the window in his favorite recliner chair. But somewhere nearby, behind closed doors, a vote was taking place. The Board of Directors of the Board of Child Care (BCC) was adding new members to its roster. The directors were about to vote in one of their own. For you see, the Strawbridge Home for Boys had become the Board of Child Care of the United Methodist Church. It was 1996, and Dad was voted in as one of the newest board members that year.

He was always a constant fixture on the BCC campus in Baltimore. He would be on hand to help out with events for the children who were residents. He volunteered to set things up, clean things up, or just be on campus to share his story. In telling his story, he would show the children that they, too, could make their dreams come to life. His tale was an inspiration to many of the children who called the BCC home.

The BCC campus was also home to the Strawbridge reunions. Just like any other family who wants to get together and stay connected, the brothers from the Strawbridge Home would meet every five years or so, have a picnic, and catch up with one another on the grounds at the Board of Child Care. The reunions couldn't be held at the original

Strawbridge Home. The Strawbridge Cottage and Carroll Building on the site in Sykesville had long since been turned into apartment buildings. The other buildings on the old farm were rented out or sold, too. Some had become private residences.

The Strawbridge Home for Boys, the old Kelso Home for Girls, and the Swartzell Home for Children had all merged into BCC over the years. Strawbridge had closed its doors to new residents in 1959. The boys who had been living there at the time were moved to BCC to live. Dad's brother Richard was one of those boys. He had spent one year at Strawbridge and then moved onto the new campus at BCC in 1959.

The BCC campus was an obvious place for all the boys to come together. At some point, Dad became head of the alumni group. As President of the Strawbridge Alumni Association, he not only organized the reunion events, but he was also the keeper of the history of Strawbridge. At every reunion he could be seen hauling two big boxes full of pictures and all the memorabilia. He would set it up on a table for the attendees to view. He had pictures of the home, the farm, and the buildings. There were pictures of the young boys when they lived there. He also had a list of all the boys who had ever called Strawbridge home with the dates they had arrived and the dates they left and moved on. He made sure the history was preserved and their stories were shared. These things were a reminder of the past they had spent together and offered the boys a chance to reminisce about the years they had been brothers.

Dad worked hard to maintain the history of Strawbridge and its influence on so many of the boys and to keep the connection intact for the boys who were now men. The efforts to maintain this large family who shared so much of their past did not go unnoticed by the board members of the BCC and its President at the time, Mr. Thomas Curcio. Given Dad's heritage and his success post-Strawbridge, they felt very strongly that he would be a great asset to their board membership and that Dad would be a strong advocate for the children's programs they had in place. He had walked in their shoes. He knew what it meant to leave your home behind and start fresh with a new beginning, a new opportunity. He could be the voice of conviction with other board members, the agencies' constituents, government groups supporting the various programs, and the Methodist church. His experience as a Strawbridge boy was invaluable. He was an incredible testament to the social services that were provided to families. The support and guidance he had received had put him on a path to a good life.

Dad couldn't believe it when they had asked him to consider being a part of the Board of Directors. He was even more amazed that they unanimously voted him to be part of the group. A boy from Bowie, a boy from Strawbridge was now going to be an integral part of the work and strategy that would benefit so many children who came to BCC for refuge, shelter, an education, and a home.

Dad did not take this leadership role lightly. He wanted to provide counsel to the committees he served and to provide guidance to the board on the direction of the agency and its services. The heritage he represented was always with him with every decision he made. His faith and purpose had been forged the day he stood on the steps of the Strawbridge Home for Boys back in 1950. He didn't know it at the time, but his fate was sealed that day.

Everything he did from that day forward had brought him to this point in his life. As he walked the campus at BCC, there was a determination in his gait. There was always a sense about him that he knew where he was going and what he was supposed to do, and it made others want to follow in his steps. It was this attitude and ability to influence that encouraged the young residents at BCC.

They knew him as Mr. Mathis. He was always impeccably dressed and wearing a smile. He always knew you only had one chance to make a good first impression. He lived by that adage. He made sure that the first one for the BCC residents was good and strong and lasting.

During the years Dad served as a board member, the Board of Child Care continued to provide for the needs of children and families. The Gaither Road campus in Baltimore also continued to evolve. In 1997, the administration building was completed, and the new Strawbridge School was completed, too. I am sure that Dad had some influence in the naming of the school. He would have been in the ear of both the board and Mr. Curcio. The three organizations that had melded into BCC—Kelso, Swartzell and Strawbridge—all had been recognized and their influence on the larger organization honored by having buildings on the campus bear the names.

The Strawbridge School began in 1994. Education was such a key influence in Dad's life, and now the Board of Child Care was going to make sure that all residents would be able to get one. The school would serve those living on the campus and those in surrounding communities who needed a different type of education system.

The education need was identified, but the building didn't yet exist. So the decision was made to repurpose some of the space in the old auditorium on campus on a temporary basis. They retrofitted the building to make it work for students and made it feel like actual classrooms. The new Strawbridge School building, as it stands today, was not opened to students until 1997.

The boys who were residents of the Strawbridge Home for Boys were always able to attend the local schools in Sykesville. However, as life became more complicated, and families and youth had to handle more traumas such as abuse and neglect, some of the children who came to BCC were not in an emotional state to handle the structure of the local schools. The New Strawbridge School allowed for customized programs and teaching to provide an education for those students who needed a different type of learning environment.

In 1995, the first graduation was held at the Strawbridge School for five of its youth. The building was not yet complete, but the mission to provide a school was in motion. The temporary school that had opened in 1994 delivered on the promise to provide education, tools, and skills for the students to begin to live independent lives.

Dad and Mom were there to see them reach this milestone. Just as Dad had set an example so long ago for his siblings and fellow Strawbridge boys, these new graduates would be able to do the same. Reaching goals, striving harder. Living the agency motto, "Hope for the future, Power in the present."

In 1997 the Board of Child Care also added seven independent living cottages on the campus. These were used for the older youth. They were taught life skills as well as their regular academic studies. In 1999, the chapel on campus was consecrated, and the campus itself was rededicated. In October of that year, there was a 125th anniversary celebration. In the beginning, the homes were created to serve the needs of families and to provide a safe place for children. By 1999, the mission was still the same. The needs of families and youth were still great, and Dad and the BCC were there to serve.

The Board of Child Care Board of Directors put a grants program in place. This allowed them to also support additional parallel programs similar in their missions and provided funding to more services to support families and children. Dad clearly would have voted to support these types of grants as they mirrored his own personal mission to help others. Work also began in the late 1990s to start to preserve the history and heritage of the entire organization. Just like Dad, the BCC at that time did not forget where it came from and how it came to be a premier service to children in need in Maryland; Washington, DC; and West Virginia. It was receiving numerous accreditations, endorsements, and recognition for its successful work.

A proposal was made to begin to organize a timeline of all the things the previous entities—Swartzell, Kelso, and Strawbridge—had accomplished and the impact they had on the communities they served. From 1959 to the present, the work that BCC was doing would also be documented. One of Dad's fellow board members, Sally Ransom Knecht, was appointed to work on this project. Dad offered his support to help her and provide guidance and context with the historical Strawbridge piece.

The Archives Building and Welcome Center, that carries Sally's name, was completed in 2006. There was a big dedication ceremony that many of the Strawbridge alumni attended. I was there, too. It was amazing to see the history and hear the stories behind all the memorabilia and pictures. You could tell that each piece, each picture, each artifact was chosen so carefully, so thoughtfully. Sally and Dad had worked on this project tirelessly for many years, and now it had come to life. The stories and history shared with the next generation, so they could pass it on.

Sally shared with me that they had started the project by sifting through many moldy boxes of papers and pictures. She was charged with organizing the data, the timeline of the historic moments in the history of the organizations, and then determining the best way to present it to the community. It was evident in the final result that both Sally and my father took great care and infused much passion into the work they did.

They were both strong believers that you cannot get to where you want to go unless you remember and appreciate where you came from. The history and heritage so lovingly documented is now accessible and available for all the residents who pass through BCC's doors. Families of the residents and visitors to the campus can also see the legacy of the organization serving their family and community. They can see who came before them and know that they, too, can leave a unique mark for their part of BCC history.

Dad remained a board member until the day he died in 2015. His dedication and commitment to the children was always unwavering. The work he was doing and the strength of character he brought to everything he did was unmatched. By 2002, his great works were recognized in an even bigger way. He was going to be asked to do more. And, of course, he said yes.

Third Week of August

The infamous camping trip to Frontier Town.
Dad, Amy, and Debbie at the campsite.
Ocean City, Maryland, 1969.

The "Wichita Lineman" may not have taken vacations, but Dad made sure that we did. He worked so hard, and at least one week out of the year, he took time off from phone work, volunteer work, and church work to take a family vacation. My father really was the physical embodiment of Clark Griswold. But, during the 1970s Dad also looked a lot like another Clark – Clark Kent. With long sideburns and black-rimmed glasses he looked like Superman's alter ego. And, we teased him about it all the time. Clark Griswold was the father character made famous in the National Lampoon *Vacation* and *Christmas Vacation* movies. Like that Clark, Dad worked himself to death at the office all year and then wanted to plan an amazing family vacation. Something that would make wonderful family memories.

When he wasn't at the office or commuting in the car to get there, Dad was working at the church or volunteering for something in the community to help others. For one week out of the year, he felt he owed it to himself and his family to take a break. Every year, always the third week of August, he attempted to relax and enjoy himself. We went on our family vacation. It wasn't Wally World, but oh, the places we would go!

As it turned out, the places we went really didn't matter. We made our fun wherever we went. However, the places were usually not too far away and most times were within a three- or four-hour drive. Places like Ocean City, Maryland, or the mountains of Virginia or sometimes West Virginia. One time, we went to the Poconos in Pennsylvania. We stayed in a pink motel that had a pool. I know that because we have pictures of it to remind me. The one picture that stands out for me is of me at the top of a hill near our hotel room. At the bottom of the hill is the pool, and Debbie is actually in the pool. I am in a lime-green pants outfit with pink flowers. I have pink yarnies in pigtailed hair. Did Mom plan this so I would match the motel? Years later, we always joked about the pink motel. If I were traveling for business, my sister would ask if the hotel where I was staying was pink.

Most of the real family vacation memories were made in Ocean City, Maryland. We went the same week every year. We had traditions that were built over time. Things like walking on the boardwalk, renting bikes to ride on the boardwalk, flying kites, feeding the seagulls, sunburns, eating boardwalk fries with vinegar, riding the old-time carousel at the Play-Land at the end of the pier, Dumser's Ice Cream, Fisher's Popcorn. The list goes on.

As I conjure up the memories, I can still smell the salty air, taste the vinegar on the fries and the sweet caramel on the popcorn. As we got older, we would sit on benches on the boardwalk and watch people go by. For some reason the boardwalk brought out all kinds of people, so people watching was like a sport. We would play a game in which we made up stories about where they were from, where they were staying, where they had been to dinner, where they were headed. It seems so lame now, but it was a night full of entertainment for us. Very cost-friendly for Mom and Dad. Kind of like a warped game of Mad Libs, but about real people.

One night during our week-long stay, we would get dressed up and go out to dinner. Nothing too fancy. Mom, Debbie, and I would wear pretty new sundresses we had bought just for the occasion. Dad would wear a nice pair of khakis and sport shirt. The shirts were always plaid. My guess is in the early years, he might have actually sported plaid pants, too. Clark through and through. I always remember going to Phillips Crab House on our last night in the early years. We eventually switched it up and went to Phillips by the Sea on the boardwalk. Later still, we went to the Wharf Restaurant, which was almost at the end of the strip near the Delaware line. Back then, the restaurant options were not as abundant as they are today, so we would wait in line for hours to enjoy a delicious seafood meal. And always, there was some type of crab. Crab soup, crab cakes, crab imperial, crab au gratin. But sometime during the vacation week, there were Chesapeake Bay steamed crabs. The more Old Bay seasoning on them, the better. Funny how now eating out and having expensive seafood is something we take for granted. We would wait all year for that one night out and dream about the taste of crab.

On one particular Ocean City vacation, Dad actually thought it would be really fun if we caught our own crabs. It would give Debbie and me something else to do besides burn to a crisp on the beach from the hot summer sun. So one morning, we went to the bay side to hang out on a pier, and we tried to catch our dinner. I actually think the memory of the day plays out better in my head than the reality of the actual day. As it happened, the day didn't really go as planned. At the start of the day, we were so excited. Mom had packed us a picnic lunch. Probably peanut butter and jelly sandwiches. Grape jelly. Or baloney sandwiches with mustard. Those were the only two sandwiches I ever remember eating when I was little. I still like them today. We had two coolers—one for our picnic and one for the crabs. Dad had bought chicken necks as our bait to catch the crabs. The only other things we needed were string and nets.

We tied the string to raw chicken necks and then sat on the pier and dropped them into the water. The chicken necks were slimy and smelled, but Dad assured us that the crabs would love them. We held on to the end of the string and let it hang over the edge of the pier. We dangled the chicken necks in the water and then just waited to see if a crab would jump on to eat. I don't remember that we had an actual crab trap. We were literally catching them by hand. With the string. Then we would try to scoop them up with the net.

I think we ended up catching about a dozen or so crabs. I'm sure the first one was so exciting. We would have screamed, "We got one!" The crab would have clung to the chicken neck as we scooped him up. Probably the second or third ones we caught, would have been exciting, too. But I am certain that about an hour into the crabbing experience, we would have started to ask, "Are we done yet? Can we go to the beach now?" And I am just as certain that Dad would have made us stay until we had caught enough for dinner, not just for an appetizer. One of his mottos—you always finish what you start.

So we probably ended up with about twenty crabs. It was enough for dinner for the four of us. We had put the crabs in our cooler and headed back to our rented beach house. We were already salivating at the thought of cracking them, crushing the claws with crab hammers, and eating them later. Smelling them cooking with Old Bay. But what Debbie and I didn't realize is that first you have to put them in the giant crab pot to cook. Alive. It's really quite barbaric. They actually scream and try to crawl out of the pot. And what Dad didn't realize is that when you catch them, in order to keep them alive until you cook them, you have to put them in salt water from the bay. Whoops! Dad had unknowingly put them in tap water in the cooler.

When we got back from the beach later that afternoon, the crabs had all died. We were not going to get to cook them and eat them. We were so disappointed. That experience was the first and last time we ever went crabbing as a family. If "crabbing with daughters" had been on Dad's bucket list, he could now check it off. We didn't need to do it again. We learned that it's much easier to just go get them already steamed and ready to eat.

Every summer after that, whenever we got crabs, we always shared the story of Ocean City. Someone at the table would invariably hold up a crab and start to say, "Remember when we tried to catch these…?" It was always good for a laugh, and we would rehash the story about how we didn't know what we were doing. Despite the fact that we were not successful, the fact that we had spent the day together doing something fun and different was enough. The memory of a great day has stuck in our heads forever.

We recently took my daughter to a pier in Oak Island, North Carolina. We took chicken necks, string, and a net. We passed our experience on. We actually didn't even catch a crab. We were close on a few of them, but they kept falling off the string before we could get them in the net. It didn't matter. Now she knows how to do it. Pop-Pop would be so proud.

It's funny that the most memorable vacation stories and the ones we share over and over again are those when things didn't quite go according to plan. The best times, the times when we laughed the most, were when things were going from bad to worse. It seemed that the badder things got, the better. And the harder we laughed about it.

One of those exact times when it seemed like one more thing could not go wrong was on our trip to Ocean City circa 1969. I was six years old. Dad thought it would be really great for us to experience camping. And I am not talking about the "glamping" that exists today. This was in a camper Dad had borrowed from his friend and fellow Strawbridge brother, Bob Bruce. One that we pulled behind the car. OK. So maybe one step better than a tent. But I am not sure why my mom ever agreed to do this.

Dad also had to borrow a car to haul the trailer. It was my uncle Jimmy's car. (Yes, we have lots of Jimmy's in our family.) Our car, a green Ford Torino, was not equipped with a hitch to tow the trailer behind it. Uncle Jimmy's car was a red Ford something or other. It was maybe a bit bigger than our car, but it was also a little bit older and a little bit beat up. It really didn't look like it could pull much of anything, much less our camper. And I think the car was actually bigger than the trailer. Where were we going to sleep?

But off we went. In a borrowed car pulling a borrowed camper, we pulled out of the driveway on Marvin Avenue to head on our camping adventure. We were staying in Frontier Town on the outskirts of Ocean City. We were so excited. The feeling didn't last very long. We got about two hours into the trip, and then the car started bucking and blowing smoke out the back and died with a big gasp on the side of the road. It should have been a sign of things to come. We should have known this was the beginning of the end of our camping fun. Uncle Jimmy's rusted-out car had to be towed to the nearest gas station. So instead of the normal three-hour trip to Ocean City, this trip turned into an all-day affair. Instead of yummy campfire food for dinner on our first night, we were eating stale crackers out of the gas station vending machines.

We finally arrived at the campsite in the dark. The trailer was so small there was barely room to breathe. The small table to use for eating also turned into a very small bed at night. I think the back seat of the car would have been more comfortable and offered more legroom. We ate outside on the wooden picnic table provided by the campsite so that we could have the full outdoor camping effect. Mom, our cheerleader of fun, would have tried to make us see that this was part of the adventure, part of doing something not in our normal routine. Eating outside in the heat with the bugs and ants and flies was all part of this Mathis Lampoon Vacation. They never show bugs in the vacation brochures. But they always seem to be on every vacation with you anyway. Especially this one.

There was no bathroom inside the camper. I am sure we had a bucket for emergencies. Sounds a bit like Bowie, now that I think about it. We had to walk to the bathhouse that had toilets, sinks, and showers. Just like when Dad was a little boy dealing with the Bowie outhouse, we did not want to have to go hiking across the campground to the bathhouse in the middle of the night. We agreed if you had to go, you were waiting until the morning.

I don't remember exactly when the rain started, but what I do know is that it rained for about six of the seven days we were on this camping adventure. It was like a tropical nightmare. It was a hundred degrees and 100 percent humidity. There were mosquitoes the size of pterodactyls. The loft bed where Debbie and I were sleeping was about six inches from the roof of the camper. At first, I thought this was going to be so cool. It so wasn't. It was claustrophobic, and with all the buzzing from the bugs, we felt like we were in the middle of a beehive. Mom was burning a hundred citronella candles to get rid of the bugs. It's a wonder we didn't pass out from the fumes. I am not sure what was worse—getting bitten and scratching to death or smelling the fumes and gagging to death. To this day the smell of citronella brings back memories of this camping trip. Maybe it is why I am not much of a camper. My sister isn't, either. I think we were completely traumatized.

With the constant rain, the beach was not really an option. But Mom and Dad wanted to make sure that we were making fun vacation memories anyway. I think it was on this particular trip that we went to Assateague Island to see the wild ponies. Debbie and I used to think it was so funny to say we were going to *Ass*-ateague, with emphasis on the first syllable. We were not allowed to say cuss words, but this was the name of the island, so we could get away with it. We were such nerds.

Watching the horses roam freely around the island and the beach was so peaceful. I am sure we had some sort of picnic there. More peanut butter and jelly. All our memories involve some type of meal or food. I am sure we had road trip snacks in the car, too. Maybe more stale crackers left from the gas station.

Since we were staying at Frontier Town, we had to visit the on-site theme park. Frontier Town was a western-themed park that had Wild West shows, Can-Can shows, Native American dancing, gunfights, bank holdups, you name it. If it happened in the west in the late 1800s, it was happening at Frontier Town. Real cowboy and Indian stuff. It sounded like a good idea and was advertised as fun for the whole family. I think it's still around today.

So on the one day it stopped raining long enough for us to go to the park, we went. Mom and Dad knew that I was deathly afraid of clowns. They really can be quite scary. I would completely freak out when we saw them at parades or at the circus. However, what they didn't know was that apparently, I was also deathly afraid of Indians. Maybe it was the headdresses they wore or the war paint on their faces that reminded me of clowns. I am not sure. But the trip to Frontier Town did not go very well. It's funny that I was so afraid of the Indians.

Dad had always been told that his family was part Native American Indian. The Poarch band of Creek Indians, to be exact. So, ironic that I was so afraid. We recently found out that the Indian story Dad had been told since he was little was just an urban legend that his grandmother had dreamed up. She thought the family was going to get rich off reservation land turned into oil land or land for casinos. Regardless, at six years old, I was not worried about being politically correct, and I was scared to death of the Indian show they did at Frontier Town. I screamed so loud that we had to leave and head back to our camp of horrors.

Years after our big camping adventure, *The Carol Burnett Show* did a sketch about a couple staying in a camper. Carol Burnett and Harvey Korman played the camping couple. It might as well have been Jimmy and Lois. I swear they had written the script based on our trip to Frontier Town. We were laughing so hard, Dad rolled off the sofa. I think that sofa was bigger than our camper.

The next several years when the third week of August rolled around, we would always head to Ocean City. Dad was doing well and making more money, so the places we stayed seemed to get a little nicer each year. One time, we stayed in a two-story condo near the beach. Then, for a couple of years, we stayed at a mobile trailer park in Montego Bay up near 145th Street. It was near Fenwick Island. Dad had worked with a guy at the phone company who owned one of the mobile homes. It was really a nice place and even had a pool.

Then one year, Dad came home with a brochure for a place in Bethany Beach, Delaware. Bethany Beach was just a little bit farther up Ocean Highway from Ocean City. The place sounded like Shangri-la. It was advertised as a private home near the beach with lots of room for the entire family and more. We were going to rent the whole house.

Debbie and Bryan were living in Kansas at this time and had planned to come join the family fun. Nicole, my niece and Debbie's firstborn, had just been born in March, and she was going on her first Ocean City family vacation. She certainly was not going to get to experience the beach in Kansas!

The brochure boasted lots of room for sleeping, a loft, and lots of amenities. It also said the house was right on the beach. It sounded great. But keep in mind this was before TripAdvisor and the age of apps and reviews. Other than going to see it in person or looking at a photo, there wasn't a way to check your destination before you went. So, basically, Dad was booking it based on the brochure and talking to the real-estate lady taking reservations for the owner. Of course, she was going to say it was great. She got a cut of the weekly rentals.

Mom and Dad thought it would be wonderful to invite my grand-mother, Nannie, and Aunt Beverly and her children and grandchildren. A giant family vacation. I was bringing one of my best friends, Valerie. We were imagining great days at the beach, hitting the clubs and dancing at night. Jumping in the surf, making sandcastles, flying kites, big feasts for the whole family at the end of the day. Lots of memories to be made and shared.

Val and I arrived first. As soon as we got there, we thought we must have been at the wrong address. We double-checked. It was right. The house was about three blocks from the beach, not actually on the beach. Now that we recall, the brochure probably said water view, not water-front. Big difference. I think if you looked out the south-facing windows and stood on your tippy toes and cocked your head just right, you might actually see a glimpse of the water. Or maybe it was just a reflection off the window next door. Either way, the beach was not right outside our door.

It also looked like it might only sleep four people, maybe six, if you were lucky. We had more than twenty people coming to stay for a week. There were only two bedrooms on the first floor. The upstairs or "roost," as we later affectionately called it, had to be accessed with a ladder. My grandmother and aunt would never make it up there. Just trying to picture them climbing the ladder made us crack up and laugh hysterically.

Then there was the delivery guy who showed up to bring a crib for Nicole. He just stood at the door trying to figure out how he was going to get the baby's bed in the house and exactly where he was going to put it once he got it in the door. There was literally no room, no floor space to put it. The bathroom was so tiny you could barely turn around or even open the door the whole way without bumping it on the sink. You had to squeeze into the corner near the sink to shut the door so you would have room to sit down on the toilet and have privacy. And, even then, your knees would touch the door. There was only a stall shower, no bathtub for the kids. The house was not built to code; it was built for munchkins.

I was wishing Val and I had stopped somewhere to get something alcoholic so we could be better mentally prepared for when my Mom and Dad arrived. When they did arrive a few minutes later, the fireworks started. Mom couldn't believe we were going to be staying in this place for a week. Dad called the rental place that had rented him this "beachfront vacation house for a large family." What was their definition of *large*? Of *beachfront*? Of *vacation*? When he had asked about laundry facilities, they had scoffed at him and said, "Who does laundry on vacation?" When he asked about the bathtub, they just suggested that we use the kitchen sink for the baby. The same sink used for washing dishes. It was insane.

Unfortunately, due to the limited space, the beds became first come, first served. My cousins and their families had not yet left home to join us, so they ended up not making the trip at all. All the beds and floor space had already been accounted for. Even with a smaller number of people than we originally planned on, we were still on top of one another. Poor Dad. We were definitely not going to forget this trip. We would definitely have memories, just not the ones Dad had planned.

We were crammed into this little space, but we made the best of it as we always did. Dad made sure of it. As we look back on that vacation now, we made lasting memories and definitely had lots of laughs. Mostly at Dad's expense. This poor man just wanted to give his family the best vacation. I am not sure he ever realized that he actually did. We were all together. We laughed a lot. We had fun in spite of ourselves. And that's all that mattered.

Sometimes Dad took vacations and long weekends that weren't always with our family. He also made time to spend with his siblings. His brothers were scattered all around the country. Sometimes they were living around the world, depending on where their military careers had taken them. Uncle Bill was in the navy, and Uncle Richard was in the army. As they got older, I think that Dad still wanted to create that closeness they had shared when they spent time in Florida every summer as kids.

For many summers, his sister Sara hosted several Mathis family reunions at her home in Britton Bay off the Chesapeake Bay in southern Maryland. The reunions were usually held on July Fourth weekend so that as many Mathis's as possible could come to celebrate on a long weekend. The festivities always included lots of sharing of stories of Oliver's children's childhood pranks and travels. We also played games—some normal like volleyball and some not, like One Hung Low.

One Hung Low was a team game in which you put a grapefruit or a croquet ball in one leg of a pair of pantyhose. Then you tied the pantyhose around your waist so that the one ball hung between your legs. You can just imagine what this looked like. Picture eight to ten grown men with this contraption strapped to their waists! Then you had to swing your hips to get a swinging action from the ball between your legs to hit a second ball on the ground toward some goal. It was hilarious and crazy and typical Mathis family fun.

The Mathis brothers learned the hard way about using a croquet ball for this game. Mathis men had skinny, birdlike legs and even skinnier ankles. After playing this game, their ankles were black and blue from the ball hitting them repeatedly. One year, they finally came up with a new way to play. They replaced the croquet ball with a grapefruit and used it to hit oranges. They no longer had to torture themselves with croquet balls.

The Mathis boys also planned brothers-only camping trips. Each summer, at least for a couple of years, they would all meet up at a campsite in southern Maryland or somewhere in Virginia. Uncle Richard would rent a pop-up tent for them to sleep in. It also had a few other amenities. He always joked you couldn't go camping without a microwave. How else did you make popcorn? After roughing it in Bowie as kids, they took advantage of small luxuries in life—like microwave popcorn. They would spend two or three days sitting around the campfire, telling stories. Go fishing and canoeing. They were recreating the adventures they had as young boys at Grandma Mathis's house. I wonder if they took hard-boiled eggs on these camping trips. My guess is they still played What's That Smell? Boys will be boys.

Each year, they would get something new to add to their camping gear. Mom and Dad started a tradition that the campers were given some kind of camp-themed item, and they had to wear it. Or else. Clearly, it was a great photo op. One year, it was Daniel Boone–style coon hats. The next year, it was frog flyswatters. The following year, it was bear masks. And so on. Each of them would bring all his gear each year and take pictures with all of it on.

One crazy year, a reporter happened to be at the campsite doing a story for the local TV station about storms in the area. She found the Mathis brothers all decked out in their coon hats and bear masks. She thought they were so silly and that their story was much more enter-taining than the weather she was sent to talk about. So they became local celebrities that night as they made the evening news. The story of four brothers taking time out of their busy lives to share fun and make wonderful memories was a story worth sharing with her audience. The real story that people should have paid attention to was that here were four brothers separated when they were little making up for lost time as adults. Spending time together, making time to laugh, and making more memories.

The Mathis brothers—Billy, Richard, Jimmy, and Ronnie—on one of their camping trips.

Retirement for most people would include perhaps a beach place, a lake place, a boat, big trips to see the world, and lots of time with family. Dad's retirement dreams were not much different. He wanted to buy an RV, travel the country, and visit family. Or, at the very least, just set up camp somewhere and enjoy the simple pleasures of life. He and Mom just wanted to see some sights and spend time with each other, maybe see family in their travels. As I think about it now, I don't think it was to create some new adventure in his life. Frankly, I am not sure why they weren't traumatized by our Ocean City camping adventure like Debbie and I. But I think he saw the retirement adventure as a way to remind himself of his childhood and the comfort of home and his family. Although his definition of comfort would definitely be questionable.

Dad worked really hard and rarely took time to relax. The vacations we took and the weekends camping with his brothers were just part of his down time. As you now know, he loved to play golf. Once fully retired, he played every Wednesday with the same group of men. They had two foursomes and would go to a different course every week, somewhere in Maryland or southern Pennsylvania. They didn't care how long it took to get there. They could take all day. They were retired. He would also play any other chance he got. He loved the game.

Some of the same guys he golfed with would also get together week-ly for breakfast. I think they would figure out what golf course they would play next and work out strategies for that elusive hole-in-one. They called themselves the "ROMEOs": Retired Old Men Eating Out. Dad always said that breakfast was one of his favorite meals. I'm sure it had something to do with his love of pig meat.

Dad also tried his hand at a few other hobbies over the years. His learning didn't stop with academic subjects. Every once in a while, he would sign up for the adult-education night classes offered through the county. We never knew what he was going to do next.

For example, when it was obvious computers were around to stay and were going to be part of all our lives, Dad took classes to learn how to use one. I think he also took a photography class, too. For some of us, taking classes may not sound relaxing, but for Dad, using his mind was better than resting it. Learning something new was always fun for him. Sometimes he didn't wait until the third week of August to go find his fun.

One time, he took guitar lessons. That led to trying to play the banjo. I wouldn't say that he had much natural music ability, but like everything else, he gave it 110 percent and tried his best. He especially liked country and bluegrass music, and he was trying to learn to play like the guys he admired who played at the Grand Ole Opry. He was a fan of singers like Hank Williams, Chet Atkins, and the Oakridge Boys. He was also a huge fan of the old TV show *Hee Haw*. Good, silly skits and good music—in his opinion, anyway. He watched it in syndication, laughing at the same jokes in the reruns over and over. If you happened to be in the room with him when he was watching, he would tell you what was coming, trying to catch his breath to tell the joke between his own laughter. It was sometimes funnier to watch him try to tell the joke than the actual joke.

However, Mom was the real musician in the family. She still is. She is the organist and choir director at Oakland United Methodist Church. She has been doing that for many years. It's hard to imagine there was ever anyone else who sat behind the organ. So, of course, Dad was in the choir, too. This was just one more thing that they did together. One more thing he did at church. He put his training from the Double Quartet at Sykesville High to work and was part of the men's section of the choir.

These days, I only attend Oakland Church on holidays and random weekends when we are visiting in Maryland. On a recent Sunday, it was actually Easter Sunday, as the choir processed into the sanctuary singing "Christ the Lord is Risen Today," it really hit me that Dad was gone. Seeing the empty space on the choir pew where Dad used to sit just made me so sad. There was a big void, and it was hard not to miss. I tried to hold it together, but I needed to step out of church to compose myself. And then at that moment, I realized he was probably singing somewhere. Singing with the angels.

Dad liked to sing. He actually had a pretty good voice. I would probably say he was a tenor. He was always singing something country or something bluegrass or humming along to anything playing on the radio. I have this very vivid memory of him singing along to the Eagles song "Take It Easy." He knew the words, or at least he pretended to. If he didn't, he just made them up. We all do that, right?

The memory is fuzzy, or maybe it was just a dream I had recently. I don't know. But we are riding in his blue Ford Falcon, all the windows down, and he is singing that song. We are on Lyons Mill Road. This is a very windy, hilly road just off Liberty Road near Randallstown, Maryland, not that far from Sykesville. We would go on rides in the car sometimes just to ride around. No destination in mind. Especially in the summer.

Many stretches of this road are covered with a canopy of trees. So when you ride down the road fast with the windows open, it feels like air-conditioning to cool you off on a hot summer day. In my memory-dream, I am not sure if it's Debbie or my best friend Cheryl in the back seat with me. I just have this vision of our hair blowing in the wind. Blond hair all tangled up with brown. We stick our heads out the window to get even more air.

When you went over the hills fast, it made your belly drop. Dad would say we were on a roller-coaster. It felt like that. I didn't get to ride a real roller-coaster at an amusement park until I was in my early twenties. It was the SooperDooperLooper at Hershey Park in Pennsylvania. The thrill of the "roller-coaster" on Lyons Mill Road somehow is much more memorable.

And I can still smell the scent of freshly cut grass as we drive on these back roads. The trees smell, too. Like earth, like dirt. Summer smells. Dad has one hand on the wheel, one hand out the window. Trying to catch the wind. The wind ripping through the car. We are all laughing. Dad is singing loudly to the radio. The dreamlike movie, as it plays in my head, is almost like he's trying to say, "Just take it easy. Don't take life so seriously." Tell a joke, sing a song, take a ride with no destination, and make time for the good times.

One of the random sentimental things that I have that was Dad's is his old Philco transistor radio. It's small, like the size of a cell phone, but about an inch thick. It's a faded shade of powder blue. When I hold it, I can remember him having it sitting in the windowsill of our garage. He would be tinkering with his cars or trying to organize a box of tools he had just bought at a yard sale. He was forever checking out yard sales or flea markets for a good deal on tools he already had. Or maybe a deal on electrical cords. How many of those does one person need? In the garage he would be singing along to the songs of the day or listening to an Orioles game. Or maybe a Colts game. Simple pleasures for a simple man. The radio doesn't play anymore. Not even static. But it is one of my most prized possessions. It was his. If I hold it tight enough to my ear, I can still hear the music. I know it's just a memory of the music playing, but it always brings tears to my eyes. And makes me smile at the same time.

The Legacy

Today I shall behave as if this is the day I will be remembered.

—Dr. Seuss

The Strawbridge Home for Boys gatepost, St. Paul's United Methodist Church, Sykesville, Maryland. Original post from 1924. Relocated to this location 2016.

Full Circle

As a member of the Board of Directors for The Board of Child Care, Dad served under several leaders who carried the title President of the Board. A gentleman named Ted Jackson had been in the role from 1993 to 1996. He was the President when Dad first became a member of the board in 1995. From 1996 to 1999, the President of the organization was Dad's good friend and BCC colleague Sally Ransom Knecht. After Sally, Dick Adams took the helm of the Board of Directors from 1999 to 2002. Then at one of the meetings in 2002, Dad was shocked that Tom Curcio, President of the agency at that time, and some of the board members mentioned something he just couldn't believe. He came home and let Mom know that they had made the suggestion to him to consider taking on the role of President of the Board of Directors. If he agreed to take on the leadership role, then he would go through the nominations process.

He just couldn't believe it. As he did with a lot of big decisions in his life, he asked Mom what she thought. He probably also called his brother Billy to see what he thought about his taking on this position. He knew this was quite an honor and a big commitment.

Of course, he was extremely humbled that a former Strawbridge boy was going to be in a potential position to lead the board of the agency that had taken care of his family so many years ago. Yes, the agency had changed over the years. It had evolved due to changing needs of families and children. But it had been resilient through those changes and had always been dutiful to the mission to serve the families and children in need and the communities where they lived.

He did not take the role or the responsibility lightly. Many of his colleagues on the board at the time said that he was a quiet, thoughtful leader. They recognized that at the heart of every decision he made was consideration of the benefit and the impact any decision would have on the children.

He was a true gentleman and a guiding star to many within the organization. He was called on to do many tasks, lead committees, evaluate plans for the agency. He worked on seeking additional grants to receive access to the necessary funds required to keep programs running. He often helped write or review them. He was even the one frequently called upon to come sign checks at the agency when needed. The staff in the finance department knew if they called Dad, he would drop everything to come take care of whatever they needed him to do.

After careful consideration, Dad accepted the nomination for President of the Board of Directors. So in 2002, a unanimous vote of the board members put him in the position. We were so proud of his work, and it was great that there was recognition for all that he had done. It was also a vote of confidence that he would continue to do more. He served as President of the Board until 2006. The usual term for this leadership position was three years. However, in 2005, Dad was asked to serve for an additional year. The organization was going through some transitions, and keeping Dad on through that work that needed to be done would maintain continuity for the agency and the board. He gladly stayed in the role to continue to lead and guide and influence the board and its work.

On the historic timeline of the Board of Child Care, there were many key events that took place under Dad's tenure as President of the Board. In 2003, the agency approved and opened the DC Early Childhood Education Center. The center still operates today with a long waiting list of children to attend. It is considered a premier service in the area and has received numerous education and child-service accreditations.

In 2004, the Strawbridge School was accredited by the National Commission for Accreditation of Special Education Services. By 2006, all the hard work and efforts to document the history of the agency and the three organizations that merged into one was culminated in the dedication celebration for the Sally Ransom Knecht Archive and Welcome

Center. This was a public testament to the history that Dad and Sally had worked so hard to preserve. Of course, our family was there to join in the celebration. Many of the Strawbridge alumni also attended, including Dad's brothers Billy and Richard. Dad beamed with pride that so many came out to share the history of the organization, especially the history of Strawbridge. A history he was part of making.

The year after Dad's death, believe it or not, the circle got just a little fuller. I was asked by the organization to consider becoming a member of the Board of Directors. I, too, was very humbled. What would Dad think? Someone would be continuing to represent the Mathis family in the organization he cared about so deeply. Frankly, I was a little scared to take on the responsibility. Could I live up to the expectations? I wanted to do it for Dad, but I also wanted to make sure that I was doing it for the right reasons. Something that I wanted to do, not just felt obligated to do. In the end, I knew it was the right step for me. I was nominated for and accepted to the Board of Directors in 2016.

I knew I was carrying on a tradition. I was doing it for me and to follow my passions. Dad's lessons had stuck and were now mine, too, to share with others. When I went to the first meeting in July 2016, I wore one of Dad's BCC pins. It was just a brass pin with a circle of children holding hands. Not worth a whole lot, but the sentimental value was priceless. It was a little poignant since it really felt like this was a full-circle moment.

I also took the folio he always used for taking notes at every meeting. I know he was with me that day. That day and every day. I am hoping to do justice to the honor I was given to be part of such a great organization whose sole mission is to support and build communities one family at a time. One child at a time. My personal goal lies with serving that motto. Dad set the expectation bar pretty high. I am doing my best to live up to it.

Finally, a Wedding for Lois and Her Jimmy

Fiftieth wedding anniversary, November 2005. The 1955 blue Chevy "limo" with Debbie, Mom, Dad, and Amy.

They said they were too young. They said it wouldn't last. But fifty years later, Mom and Dad had proven "they" were very wrong. They were still going strong. We had celebrated their twenty-fifth anniversary in 1980 and their fortieth anniversary in 1995. For their twenty-fifth anniversary, we held a surprise party at my sister's townhouse in Columbia, Maryland. It was a small family affair with a few friends there, too, to share the special day.

For their fortieth anniversary, we decided to celebrate with a 1950s-style sock hop at the Oakland Church hall, complete with a fifties-style diner menu. This is the same hall where Dad had taught Sunday school, had parties for the youth he mentored in MYF, and served hundreds of oyster dinners to raise funds for the church. Now it was a place to celebrate forty years of life and love.

Dad and Mom were so surprised. We had tricked them into thinking they were going to some event for the church. We had a jukebox with fifties music so the guests could dance to tunes from the likes of The Platters, Perry Como, and Bill Haley and His Comets. Everyone was doing the jitterbug or the twist. Well, at least they were trying to. It was really a fun night. Dad even wore his old Sykesville High School letter sweater. Mom wore a poodle skirt. Forty years of memories had been made, and on this night, they shared them with everyone they loved.

The fifties-diner-style cuisine included such favorites as meat loaf, macaroni and cheese, and mashed potatoes. Yummy comfort food. Dad always requested meat loaf for special occasions, especially for his birthday dinner. He loved it. And of course, there were leftovers the next day to make meat-loaf sandwiches. When he and Mom had first met, she thought meat-loaf sandwiches were gross. Who ate it cold? But now when we make it, we always make two loaves—one to eat hot for dinner and one to eat cold as sandwiches. The weird part is that when it's hot, we eat it with ketchup, and when it's cold, we use mustard. Dad trained our taste buds to eat it just like he liked it. It's the one leftover I will admit to eating and liking.

In 2005, Dad and Mom reached the milestone of their fiftieth wedding anniversary. This was a big one. An even more special one. The golden one! Debbie and I decided it was high time after all these years together that they had a real wedding. The full deal. We wanted to plan a wedding ceremony to renew their vows and a real reception to celebrate and then send them off on a bona fide honeymoon trip.

They had been through enough of our weddings. Well, OK, enough of my weddings. Yes, I will admit I have had a few more than some people.

It just took me a few times to find the right one. Debbie found the right one on the first try. Mom and Dad did, too. They had raised their two girls, and by 2005 they were grandparents to Debbie's two girls. They had been through life's ups and downs and celebrations and suffered heartaches over the years, too. All the things that happen over the course of a lifetime. A lifetime spent together.

A wedding of their own was something they had never really experienced. They probably never thought it would or could happen. Maybe they didn't think it was necessary. I don't think that they ever regretted or fretted about it as something they had missed out on. Debbie and I definitely thought it was, and fifty years were definitely reason to celebrate. But how do you plan something that big and try to keep it a surprise? We kept it a secret for as long as we could. We knew if we had most of the details planned and in place, then they could not say no.

We sent the invitations to all their friends and family. We planned the reception at the church hall. Again! We worked with the pastor at Oakland United Methodist Church at the time, Reverend Mary Ellen Glorioso. She helped us choose the service, the vows, the scripture readings, and the music. We planned a honeymoon trip so they could go away for a few days after the big party.

We even got a friend to lend his vintage car for the occasion. It was a 1955 blue Chevrolet, and it would serve as their "limo." We thought it would be so great to take a literal ride down memory lane. In this case, not just a literal ride, but an actual ride. It was so cool! They went to the church in style. The golden celebration was attended by all their family and close friends. Mom and Dad were like giddy teenagers again and had the nervous jitters a bride and groom experience on their wedding day. It was perfect!

At the reception we surprised them with a honeymoon trip to the Brandywine Valley in southeastern Pennsylvania. They were going to stay at a little bed-and-breakfast place called The Chadds Ford Inn. We had made plans for them to visit wineries, tour Winterthur and Longwood Gardens, check out battlefields and the Andrew Wyeth Gallery. It was a special long weekend to celebrate their very special fifty years together.

In hindsight, I wonder if a repeat trip to Richmond would have been more fitting. Recreate that November night so long ago. Two teenagers headed on a new adventure. They had no idea where it would lead them. Fifty years later, it was so special to witness the love that had endured. And how much fun they had just being together.

**Fiftieth Wedding Anniversary Party. November 2005.
Cutting the cake and dancing to the "Chicken Dance."**

Another difference with this wedding was that Mom and Dad were not going to be registered anywhere and certainly were not expecting gifts. After fifty years of living together and collecting treasures from yard sales and flea markets, they did not need one more thing. The basement, garage, and shed were full of enough treasures gathered over the years. Dad lived by the old adage that one man's trash is another man's treasure. And Dad never got rid of anything. Everything was a treasure to him.

By this time, November of 2005, Dad was also an integral part of the Board of Child Care. He had been a board member since 1995 and President of the Board of Directors since 2002. He had mentored and guided so many children through church and through involvement with programs at BCC. It was time to set up something that would help the children and provide lasting educational opportunities in his lifetime and beyond.

During the fiftieth anniversary party, at the wedding reception, we shared stories of Mom and Dad's lasting love. Debbie and I had written our customary poem for the occasion. It's a family thing. We can't help ourselves. We feel compelled to document life events in a rhyming pattern. We had also called upon Mr. Thomas Curcio, President of the Board of Child Care at the time, to say a few words and share a very special gift of giving that had been set up for this occasion to honor Dad and Mom.

Mr. Curcio had always been a big fan of Dad. He had been influential in Dad's initial nomination to the board and further had suggested he become President of the Board. As a family, we had decided the anniversary party was the perfect time to present this gift to them.

Mr. Curcio shared how he had worked with Dad for years. He had witnessed Dad's work with children and families first hand. He had seen Dad's leadership with the staff at the agency and with his colleagues on the board. Mr. Curcio had learned the history of Strawbridge first hand from Dad. He had seen Dad's unending passion to provide for others. He knew Dad's constant support of education and pursuit of a lifetime of learning. He had such a respect for this man who had walked the walk. He then announced that Jim and his family had decided it was time to set up a scholarship fund for the children at BCC and the Strawbridge School.

The Jim and Lois Mathis Scholarship Fund was established. The first recipients of the scholarship awards would be in the graduating class of

2006. The Mathis legacy was created that night as we celebrated Dad and Mom's commitment to each other. The scholarship recipients would need to maintain an academic standard but would also have to show a commitment to their community. Give back what they had been given. This was Dad's way of preserving his passion and making sure that it would carry on. So rather than the standard wedding gift, like a vase or kitchen gadget, the wedding guests could contribute to the scholarship fund to honor what was important to Mom and Dad.

This scholarship fund continues today. Numerous scholarships have been given out over the years. Dad and Mom attended every graduation together. Celebrating this milestone event with the children meant a lot to Dad. He was there to give the deserving students their scholarships, shake their hands, and encourage them to reach for their dreams. Just like he did. He wanted to know their story and share his own. Always making sure they knew that they could do whatever they wanted in life. Inspiring them to pursue their dreams. Guiding them to lead the way for others.

The first year after Dad passed away, Debbie and I attended the graduation ceremony along with Mom and Uncle Bill. Awarding the scholarship without Dad there was incredibly hard and emotional. But that's what it is all about. We had to continue what had been started. His legacy would carry on. The good work that he put in motion will continue. The hope is that the funds will provide the means and the opportunity for the students to reach their dreams. It will encourage them to reach them, surpass them, and then inspire the next generation to go after their own.

Over the years the fund has grown. Many contribute on holidays to honor Dad. Some funds are received from church members. Some come in from family members. Some come from Strawbridge brothers to show their appreciation and respect for Dad. Some of the funds are from people who are complete strangers to us, but we know they weren't to Dad. Jim Mathis touched them in some way, and they want to honor him in a similar way. It doesn't matter where it comes from. We are just making sure that the work he set out to do will continue. Live on in perpetuity. Into the future.

And the Scholarship Goes to...

For some children, the dream of going to school and getting an education is sometimes still just a dream. They are not sure it will ever come true. I think when Dad was twelve and his world was dramatically turned upside down, he probably thought he, too, would never get to finish high school, let alone go to college. He dared to dream, and with the aid of services through the Strawbridge Home for Boys and the Methodist Church and lots of hard work on his part, his dream came true.

Dad knew that an education could open doors to new opportunities. An education was the catalyst to opening your mind to new directions and possibilities. Whether it was academic or vocational training, he wanted to make sure that other children would be given the same ability that he was given to explore their capabilities.

As a Strawbridge alumnus, Dad was part of a group of men who had been raised through Strawbridge and nurtured by their housemother, Miss Alice Seymour. The alumni had decided that the best way to honor Miss Seymour was to put a scholarship fund in place that would provide funds to help cover educational expenses for a deserving child. The scholarship funds could help cover tuition and buy books or a laptop for a student who had the academic aptitude, but not the financial means, to pursue higher education. Whatever the need, they wanted to provide a way to help cover the cost.

When the scholarship was launched, Russell Barr, a former Strawbridge boy and a good friend of Dad's, was the President of the Strawbridge Alumni Association. Dad had worked with Russell and other fellow alumni to set up the scholarship fund. In 1997, Dad became the President of the Alumni Association, and he made sure that the Alice Seymour Scholarship Fund remained in place and carried out the mission to provide the means for BCC residents to reach their educational dreams. Many of the Strawbridge alumni initially contributed to bring the fund to life. Some of them who are still around continue to fund it today. Many deserving BCC students have furthered their education with the Alice Seymour awards given each year. Dad knew she would be so proud of her boys and their commitment to promoting education.

The first James and Lois Mathis Scholarships were given in June 2006. Each year, two students are given scholarships to help with their educational expenses. The Mathis scholarship considers students who have reached certain academic achievements with the added caveat that they have also contributed to their community in some meaningful way. Dad and Mom wanted this second piece to be part of the requirements so that the scholarship recipients were aware of what it meant to be part of something bigger than themselves. It was important to Dad that, in addition to having the academic acumen, that the scholarship award winners were grateful for what they had been given and understood the need to give back. Just like Dad did.

Since 2006, more than twenty-four Mathis scholarships have been provided to twenty-four BCC residents graduating from public schools or from the Strawbridge School on site at the BCC campus. Each year, the leadership team at BCC nominates or recommends the deserving students for the scholarships. Dad and Mom attended every graduation at BCC for as long as I can remember. When the Mathis scholarship became part of the ceremony, it was even more special for them. For the first eleven years of the scholarship's existence, Dad and Mom were there to personally award the students, congratulate them on their achievement, and inspire them to soar to greater heights. The 2016 ceremony was the first one for which Dad was not present, but his spirit lived on in the expectation of students who will pursue their dreams and preserve his legacy to help others reach their goals.

As I was shaking the hands of the students who received the scholarships in 2016, I couldn't help thinking about the Strawbridge boy who had pursued his dreams, reached heights he never thought were possible, and did all that he could to pass on his wisdom for living a good life. I thought that it would be interesting to reach out to those who had received a scholarship and see where they were today. Were they pursuing their dreams? Were they helping others? I was able to meet with a few of them and capture their stories.

One of the scholarship winners in 2015 was Trevion S. He was probably one of the last to receive the Mathis scholarship directly from Dad's hands. Trevion, or Tre as he likes to be called, had arrived at the BCC campus when he was in his middle teen years. His path to BCC was a windy one.

Tre's life had started in the Lone Star State of Texas. He then lived in New Orleans, Louisiana; Atlanta, Georgia; and finally, Maryland. He had been born in Texas, but early on, there was trouble at home, and he was sent to live with an aunt and uncle in New Orleans. Then Hurricane Katrina hit. The family survived the hurricane, but their home and belongings were destroyed, so they relocated to Mississippi for a while to recover from the trauma of the storm.

When Tre was ten, his mom came back into his life. She was now back in Texas. He went to live with her for a few years, but by age twelve, he was sent to live with his aunt and uncle again. This time, they were living in Atlanta. Because of growing tension in the home and Tre's inability to do well in school, the family sought a new living arrangement for him. At this point in his life, he had lived with his aunt and uncle longer than with his mother. A stepfather who had been part of the family picture was now living in Maryland, and he offered to take Tre. Perhaps a new location would help him. Tre had anger issues and a lack of stability and now was being sent to yet another home.

Once in Maryland, the situation did not improve. So the family took the advice of local child welfare services, which offered BCC as a solution.

Tre arrived at BCC at age sixteen and first lived in Cottage 7 on the campus. He hated it at first. His first impressions were that his family had disowned him and now he was in this new, horrible place. He picked fights and struggled with his growing anger. He lashed out at those living in the cottage with him and to those trying to help him.

The counselors and program coordinators at BCC soon realized that Tre had a lot of capability, but he needed to be nurtured and guided on how to control his emotions and reactions to others. The emotional trauma of numerous parental figures in his young life had been too much to take. Each time he moved, there were new people, new rules. He needed focus and structure.

Through counseling and a structured environment, he soon began to thrive. After several months and noted improvements in his coping skills, he was allowed to attend public school. He went to Chesapeake High School in Essex, Maryland. This school was located about forty minutes away from BCC, so it was a long ride to and from school every day. It gave him a lot of time to think. He realized the importance of getting an education, and he was starting to see a future for himself. He was taught that resilience combined with patience equaled strength. The strength to deal with anything that came your way.

He completed the necessary requirements to get his high-school diploma. While doing the necessary work to graduate, he also became a role model for other BCC residents and was able to help other kids when they were in a crisis. He learned the importance and the control to talk about your problems and work them out logically rather than resorting to violence. He continued to be a mentor to the many residents at BCC as he transitioned to independent living.

At the 2015 BCC graduation ceremony, Tre received the Mathis scholarship. He was so proud of his accomplishments. He had family there to support him. They had been through some difficult times, but now the future looked pretty bright. His mom, aunt, and uncle were all there to congratulate him.

Tre was accepted into an eight-month hybrid program through the State Highway Commission and Community College of Baltimore County. He planned to study computer-aided design, welding, and construction management. Upon completion of the program, he will continue on to get his associate's degree and then enter Morgan State University to study engineering. Given that he received a Mathis scholarship, that seems so right. He intended to use the funds he received to get the laptop he would need for his studies.

In addition to his schoolwork and mentoring of other students, Tre worked on the BCC campus in the facilities department. Mr. Glenny, the work coordinator on the campus, took Tre under his wing. Tre was very persistent in pursuing a position with the housekeeping and maintenance group so he could learn another vocation while completing his studies.

While living on the BCC campus, Tre moved from Cottage 7 to House 6 and then House 9. I asked Tre where he would be living now that he was going to college. He said that he had been approved for independent living and that he was currently living in the Mathis House. Really? The Mathis House was part of the Gateway Program that allowed those approved to live independently on the campus. This house had been named for Dad back in 2012. The irony was that here was this young man who had been given a place to live and an opportunity to pursue his dream. Whether he realized it or not, a man he never really knew had made it happen. The parallel story was not lost on me. Dad had lived a life and had put things in place that were making it happen for this young man. And I knew just talking to him that Tre would someday do the same thing for someone else. Tre has since moved back to Atlanta to be with family and continue his path to complete school and find ways to give back to his community.

With all the scholarship winners over the years, I am sure many have stories to tell. All the winners shared a common theme. Young lives broken somehow, damaged youth in some way, and then the BCC was there to save them. The BCC had provided the services and healing needed to get their lives on a track—a safe, productive, self-fulfilling track. The individuals would persevere and work hard. Set goals and meet them. They would be forever grateful and want to help others in the same way.

Another story like that was the life of Crystal B. Crystal had been verbally abused and bullied at school. She had been physically abused at home. By the age of thirteen, she felt her only way to escape was to take her own life. Fortunately, she was not successful, and an intervention took her from her home to try to save her. She was then placed into foster care. It was at one of the foster homes that she was sexually assaulted. By the age of fifteen, she arrived on the doorstep of BCC a very broken teenager.

It was 1996, and Crystal was living in Cottage 4 with fourteen other girls. She had a long road to recovery ahead, and the programs to try to heal her were put in place immediately. She had a treatment team to help her through the emotional and physical trauma. She had counseling services. She was given a set of daily activities and expectations to give her life structure and routine. She was safe.

Crystal attended the BCC's Strawbridge School. She continued her studies there and completed the ninth and tenth grades. While completing her academic studies, she was part of daily therapy sessions. It was in these sessions that the real healing began, and she was able to start to process all that had happened to her in her young life.

She started to do things other teens get to do. She participated in the recreational and group activities provided on the campus. BCC offered soccer, basketball, and even had a swimming pool. She joined the softball team and still proudly displays her winning team's softball trophy.

By 1997 Crystal had been doing well in her classes at the Strawbridge School. She was sixteen. She had been accepted and was about to transition to Pikesville High School, one of the local public schools BCC residents could attend. She felt her life was gaining more normalcies day by day. Through support of the BCC and the auxiliary, she got to go to the junior and senior proms and was able to purchase things like a school ring and senior year photos. These things may sound like small things to some people. But for kids like Crystal, these small things had never seemed possible. Now she was seeing the life ahead of her very differently than the life she had left behind.

In the summer of 1998, Crystal graduated to BCC's independent living program and was able to get a part-time job. The BCC programs were preparing her to live life on her own. Crystal graduated from Pikesville High School in 1999. She was accepted to Loyola College in Baltimore. While a student there, she continued to work full or part time, depending on what her school schedule would allow. BCC helped her pay for her text books and covered her utility bills while she was living in a studio apartment near the school. School was difficult, but she never lost sight of her dream to finish. And at the age of twenty-four, she graduated from Loyola College with a degree in psychology.

Crystal was not a recipient of a Mathis scholarship. It was not yet in place when she graduated. However, I learned that she was the recipient of an Alice Seymour scholarship, and Jim Mathis would have been a part of determining who got those awards. And further, in 2005 when Crystal graduated, she found out that the BCC had decided to satisfy all her outstanding education loans. At that time, Dad was the President of the Board of Directors and would have been instrumental in the decision to make this happen. Crystal was and is forever grateful that the BCC was there to support her every step of the way. She also wishes that she could thank Mr. Mathis personally for the role he played in making her dreams come true. For helping her to reach goals she never thought were possible.

After graduation from Loyola, Crystal spent ten years working at the Johns Hopkins Behavioral Pharmacology Research Unit. (Fitting, since Hopkins was Dad's alma mater.) She is now the Program Director at Bello Machre, a nonprofit organization that provides a lifetime of loving care to adults with developmental disabilities. Since January 2006 she has been spending her Saturday's working with a young man who has low-functioning autism. She finds a lot of personal satisfaction in being a part of improving his quality of life. She sees the need to help others just like others stepped in to help her when she needed it. Different paths, but a similar story. I know Dad would be so proud to know he had helped her in some small way. I know she is grateful that he did.

Crystal's life has another parallel to Dad's. She was asked and then nominated to be part of the Board of Directors at BCC, too. She is now actively working with the organization to make sure that the mission that saved her will continue to save others. She travels throughout Maryland and visits Methodist churches to share her story and spread awareness for the BCC programs. The awareness ultimately helps to raise funds to provide support for many of the programs. Her intersection with Dad's path put her on her own path to a successful life. Now she is doing the same. Her story will motivate and lead someone else to choose success.

I know there are many other scholarship winners and many other stories. These are just a few excerpts from the lives of those who have been touched by Dad's life. Although Dad is gone, the scholarships will live on and continue to provide a way to help young lives reach their potential. Jim Mathis definitely reached his. He exceeded even his own expectations. Here's hoping that future scholarship recipients will set the bar even higher. Dad lived his life by example every day. How could you choose to follow that example? How could you choose to set your own example for others? How do you want be remembered? What will people say about you? Make sure you like the answers. Make sure you are living your life today in that way. People will not remember you for your career or the things that you bought or collected. They will remember experiences, remember the time you spend with them and your actions helping them or others.

Tribute to a Strawbridge Boy

Dad did not seek recognition for all the good work he did. In fact, he was often humbled by people paying attention to what he just did as the normal course of his life. He had surpassed the goals he had set out to achieve and probably achieved some that he never thought possible. His family, his work, his education, his commitment to church and community were all testaments to the man he was and chose to be. The work he did for the Board of Child Care were some of his proudest moments. Not for himself, but for those around him and for the children he felt he was guiding.

After Dad had served as President of the Board of Directors at BCC, he continued to be part of the executive team and was an emeritus member of the board until he passed away in 2015. In 2012, a committee for the organization was charged with making recommendations for the naming of some of the key buildings on the campus. The decision was made that the Gateway Program that supported independent living would name one of the homes the Mathis House in honor of James O. Mathis. The dedication ceremony for this honor celebrated all that Dad had done to support the organization and his undying commitment to the mission of the agency and the children it served.

Naming the independent living quarters after Dad was so appropriate. They indicated at the ceremony that this honor was being bestowed on him as he had been a resident of Strawbridge and had been President of the Strawbridge Alumnae. He had served on too many committees to count that carried out the mission to help children. The committee that was giving Dad this honor may not have realized that Dad always thought it was important to give children the means and the tools to learn to do for themselves.

He was always quoting one of the scripture lessons about how if you give someone fish they will not go hungry, but they will come to depend on the constant gift and expect the gift to be given freely. If you teach them to catch their own fish, they will also not go hungry, will have pride in their ability to provide, and will always have food for life. It's a strong message that has so many meanings and implications. It was not lost on Dad or our family that giving children a sense of independence builds strong, confident children. The Mathis House, a place to learn independent living, is a lasting tribute to the man, his work, and his lessons.

The Mathis House dedication in 2012. The Gateway Program House was named after James O. Mathis. The plaque on the house indicates the name, and Dad also received an honorary plaque to take home.

It's been almost three years since Dad passed away. It's hard to believe he is not here. In some ways he is more here now than he ever was. His thoughts and actions are with me always. I often think about the way he would say things, do things. The legacy he left behind will be lasting. Even a year after he passed, we continued to hear from long-lost friends who were just hearing about his death. They couldn't believe he was gone, either. He was such a source of strength. He was a leader in so many ways. We had no idea how many people would come out to pay their respects to him.

Dad's funeral was held at Haight Funeral Home. The Haight Funeral Home has been in business in Sykesville, Maryland, for more than six generations. The business of dying in Sykesville has always been taken care of by someone from the Haight family. They were also family to us on Mom's side. My great-grandmother was Belle Everette Haight. My daughter, Everette, is named after her. I always loved her middle name. The Haight family who ran the funeral home were distant cousins. Two or three times removed, but still family, and we knew they would take care of Dad with the grace and respect he so deserved.

Dad died on a Tuesday. We set up two viewing services for the Friday that followed, and the funeral service would take place on that Saturday. There were some in our family who had to travel to make it to Sykesville for the services, so we needed to wait a few days. The first viewing was from 2:00 p.m. to 4:00 p.m. on Friday. The second was from 7:00 p.m. to 9:00 p.m. We knew a lot of people were shocked what had happened to Dad.

It's not necessary now to go into the details of his death. Let's just say he did not get the best of care and had things been different, we might not have gone through this at this point in his life. I know everyone has to go through it at some point. You know, that whole death-and-taxes thing. It's inevitable. It was just too soon for Dad. It was not fair. Whenever we said stuff like that, Dad always said, "Life's not fair. The fair is over in Timonium." He was referring to the Maryland State Fair, maybe recalling our 4-H days. Regardless, his leaving us really wasn't fair, but here we were at this place at this time anyway.

When the doors to the funeral home opened that Friday afternoon, we had no idea the sheer volume of people who would come to see our family and pay their respects to Dad. People waited in line almost two hours just to see us. The first viewing was to end at 4:00 p.m., but we didn't leave until almost 6:00 p.m. Mom was exhausted, emotionally and physically. We all were. And we had to do it all again at 7:00 p.m. By the end of the night, more than five hundred people had come to share stories about Dad and how he had touched their lives, tell us how great he was, how sad they were he was gone. They didn't need to tell us. We were, too.

Months later, as I reflected on the people who came to see us and the stories they shared, I realized that Dad probably had no clue how many people were so grateful for him and his life. It wasn't about doing a lot of things or even big things for one person. It was about doing all the little things that no one pays attention to for so many. So, so many. He was always lending a hand to whoever needed it. And he always did it with a smile. That forever twinkle in his blue eyes. That's what everyone remembered.

The day of the funeral, Haight's was prepared for many of the people who had come for the viewing to come back for the funeral service, too. The service was held at Haight Funeral Home in their chapel rather than in a traditional church venue. Our family church, Oakland United Methodist Church, was too small and would not be able to hold all the people. Even at Haight's, it was standing room only. Nicole spoke about her Pop-Pop and pig meat. I spoke about a very special father. Bill Bruce, also a Strawbridge boy, spoke about a very special brother. Sally Knecht from the Board of Child Care spoke about an inspirational leader. The service was beautiful and paid tribute to the man and to a life well lived.

The graveside service was going to be at Old Oakland Cemetery. That's where Dad and Mom had the family grave plots and where they planned to spend eternity. Almost all Mom's family is buried there, too.

In order to get there, the funeral procession from Haight's would normally have traveled toward Liberty Road, crossing over Liberty Lake. But Haight's knew the procession would be long. On a busy Saturday, when people in town were out shopping and running errands, this normal travel pattern would not work. It would tie up traffic for miles. So they had arranged for police to stop traffic at the major intersections. I think there were at least three intersections we had to go through that morning. We crossed the big one (that's how we refer to it) at Liberty Road, continuing west until we got to what is known as Pine Knob Road. We were going to take the back way to get to the cemetery.

As we drove this route, I remember vividly as we passed by Old Bennett Road how it was so fitting that Dad was being taken along this road. A road he had traveled so many years ago. We had to go past the site of the old Strawbridge Home for Boys farm. At least, where the farm used to be. Where it had all started. Life's beginnings and endings. It all just seemed to fit. Then I happened to look to the left, and I noticed that the only thing left standing of the old Strawbridge Home that was visible from the road was the old stone gatepost. It was the original entrance to the home. I remember thinking that Dad had passed through those gates once, so long ago. And it had changed his life and the lives of those around him forever. And here we were today, and perhaps he was passing through a different set of gates. You know, the pearly ones. And it was changing our lives again. Forever. Maybe I was reaching and trying to find meaning, but it all just seemed so poetic.

I remember wondering what would happen to that gatepost if they ever decided to widen the road in the name of progress and growth in Sykesville. Some contractor would be hired to tear down the stone posts, and the community would never know about this special place or the special boys who were raised there. One in particular. I decided right then and there that I was going to do something about that. Do something so people would know. So the boys would be honored and remembered.

After the funeral, I dove headfirst into the project of saving the gatepost. I just wasn't exactly sure where to start. I needed to find out who currently owned the land where the post stood. So first I checked with county land records. I called the local historical society. I did more research and more digging. I found out that the land was actually owned by the Grimes family, but it was held in a trust for that family. I contacted the attorneys managing the trust and sought approval from them and the family to move the gatepost. They didn't have any feelings about the gatepost and didn't care if it was torn down and moved. I had crossed the first hurdle.

Then I needed to find out from the Maryland state roads department if there were any plans for any work to be done on this section of Route 32. If there were plans, would the state roads contractors be moving the stone gatepost or destroying it? Again, more research and more inquiries. I found out that there were plans to widen the road at some point, but it was in the distant future, and budgets to do it still needed approval. I knew that would take time, and I did not want to wait for them. I finally received the approval of the Maryland state roads department to have the post removed. At our expense, of course.

Next came the process of where to move it to and where its final resting place would be. I initially started the conversation with the leadership at BCC to put the gatepost on the Baltimore campus. I was thinking that it might make sense to have it be part of the Archives Building. A part of the lasting history of the Strawbridge Home. But after much consideration and conversation, it was agreed that there was a much more logical place for the gatepost. Our family and some of the Strawbridge alumni thought it would make more sense for the gatepost to remain in the community, to be a part of the town of Sykesville.

This was going to be an honorary monument to all the Strawbridge boys. They grew up in Sykesville and had called it home for many years.

Some, like Dad, had never left. The boys and the home were part of the fabric of the community. Their history had been created there. Remembering that history should be there, too.

Through connections in town, I was put in touch with Pat Greenwald of St. Paul's United Methodist Church. That was the church the boys had attended. Pat was the historian of the church, and she was also connected with the management of the town of Sykesville and the Carroll County Historic Commission. As this was something historic, she became interested in preserving it, too.

Pat worked diligently to get the church trustees interested in preserving this piece of history. She convinced them to approve the final resting spot for the gatepost. The trustees approved a location on the front lawn of St. Paul's Church. It would be part of the church grounds but would also be positioned next to the sidewalk of Main Street in Sykesville. This way, anyone visiting the town would be able to see it and read about what it was and what it meant to the community.

The entire process to get the proper forms completed, the necessary approvals, the removal of the original stone post from its location on Route 32, and rebuilding the gatepost in its new home took a little over a year. There were so many involved in the project and so many people to thank for helping get it done. Finally, on October 9, 2016, the dedication ceremony took place at St. Paul's United Methodist Church. That Sunday also served as a Strawbridge alumni reunion. About nine of the original boys attended, and more than 150 people came from the community to see the gatepost unveiled.

Many had worked tirelessly to make this happen. The idea had come to me on the day of Dad's funeral on that fateful drive to the cemetery, and now it had come to life. It was a tribute to all the Strawbridge boys, to all who had called Strawbridge home, and to all they had contributed over the years to the town of Sykesville. The home had given them a foundation and opportunity. Many of the boys became very successful men – engineers, pilots, a navy admiral, teachers and educators, and even a Pulitzer-prize winning playwright. This celebration was to show honor and respect to their heritage and the memories they created there. But truthfully, my inspiration for and dedication to making this project happen and to preserving a piece of the history was to pay homage to just one of the boys. Dad.

The gatepost dedication ceremony was a second posthumous honor for Dad. In July of 2016, Dad had been honored by the state of Maryland. He had been nominated by the BCC and the Strawbridge School to receive the Maryland Association of Nonpublic Special Education Facilities (MANSEF) Distinguished Citizen Award. We found out in May of the same year that his nomination had been considered, and Dad was hands down the obvious choice to be presented with the award.

The award is given to someone who encapsulates everything Dad believed in and lived for. It's about the children and providing education and opportunity for them. It's about providing a safe environment for them to learn. It's about providing a home for them to feel love and respect and grow into the type of people they can be and deserve to be. The world needs more people like that. Dad was given those things and felt very strongly that he could help provide them for others in similar situations. The fact that he received this award posthumously was bittersweet, but it did not minimize his ability to provide an example to those who are coming after him. His legacy of giving and helping others will live on. As a family we were there to celebrate this tremendous honor and accept the award on his behalf. And as a family, we are making sure his legacy lives on.

As you can imagine, our family was so honored for Dad to get this award and the other recognitions he has received since he had passed. They were all very bittersweet. But we also agreed that he would think they were so silly. He did not do the things he did for others to take notice. He did not want his name in lights. But each of these events made the local paper, and that is exactly what happened. His story was special and needed telling. He would think that it's crazy that I have written this book about him. He just did what he did because he didn't know to do anything different. If someone needed anything, he was there to provide it. Like the Nike ad says, "Just do it." That was Dad. He just did it.

I had talked a little bit about that part of his personality in my eulogy at his funeral. We always joked that when something needed fixing, Dad would say, "Just jiggle it!" Sometimes that actually worked to get whatever wasn't working to work again. I joked at his funeral that just like Dad used to say, "Just jiggle it," we should start a movement to honor him. I suggested, what if in performing random acts of kindness, or even the intentional acts of support for people, that we say instead, "Just Jimmy it." You know, sort of like fixing things, but instead you were fixing something for someone, doing something for them. Fixing their lives or making it better or easier for them.

Then the phrase morphed. We coined the phrase "doing a Jimmy deed." Jimmy deeds were happening all around us. Anytime someone was doing something for someone else, we would say, "I just did a Jimmy deed!" It could be anything. Take someone a meal when they are sick. Pick up their medication from the pharmacy. Help them plant flowers. Help clean their yard. Take them to the doctor. Pick up their groceries. Just stop by and let them know you are thinking about them. Show that you care. Any little thing that will make their life a little brighter, touch them in a way they will remember. Lives that Dad had touched were looking for ways they could spread the kindness he had bestowed on them. The thoughtfulness. The Jimmy-ness.

As you think about someone in your neighborhood or community who might need a helping hand, what could you do for them? What Jimmy deed would they appreciate? If everyone who could think of one way to do a Jimmy deed for someone else, the world could be a kinder, softer, gentler place. No matter what the person needs, something big or something small, just do it. Dad lived his life that way every day. Some things in his life were out of his control. But this need in him to give to and to do for others was a choice. In this small way, he chose to do things for others that they may not have been able to do for themselves. It's a choice we all should make. Go do something for someone else. Then do it again, and so on and so on. Do you get it? Have you got it? What will people say about you? Make sure it's something good! Ask yourself, "What would Jimmy do?" Now, just go do something for someone else. Go do a Jimmy deed. Just Jimmy it. Just give of yourself. Just give. Make sure you live your life so that the first word people use to describe you is *giving*.

Last Words

Carve your name on hearts, not tombstones.
A legacy is etched into the minds of others
and the stories they share about you.

—Shannon L. Alder

MEMORIAL DAY WEEKEND of 2015 would end up being the last time Nick, Everette, and I did something all together as a family with Mom and Dad. We were celebrating Mom's birthday that weekend. It was May 22, and she was turning seventy-eight. Dad had turned seventy-eight that February. The stage version of *The Lion King* had come to Philadelphia and was playing at the Kimmel Center in Center City. We had bought tickets to take Everette to see the show. However, the rest of us had never seen the show, either. We knew the story from the books and the animated Disney movie. But the Broadway show was said to be spectacular. And it was!

We didn't have the best seats. I had paid a pretty penny for them, but we were still pretty high up and had to strain our necks to look around a pole that was in the way of the stage. Of course, there was a pillar right in front of Dad's seat. But once the show started, we all stopped complaining. The music, the sets, the animals of the African plains coming to life on stage were absolutely amazing. The best part was the look on Everette's face. She lit up as soon as the curtains opened. The show lived up to all the reviews it had received over the years. We loved it.

What strikes me now, as I think back on the show and the music, are the parallels in the story about the young lion cub, Simba, and his relationship with his father, Mufasa. I am reminded of the one I had with my own. Young Simba realizes that he cannot escape who he is or where he came from and that his father is a part of everything he does. I now feel that way every day.

There is a song in the show called "He Lives in You." The lyrics tell about how there is no mountain too great to climb. In the scene in which this song is sung in the show, young Simba is looking at his reflection in a small pool of water in the jungle. The words of the song talk about how "He lives in you, he lives in me, he watches over everything we see." My sister Debbie says that sometimes now when she looks in the mirror, she sees Dad's reflection looking back at her. She should. She has his eyes. I have Mom's, so I don't see him. But I feel him. I wonder if in all the things I am doing, and have done since he passed, are the reflections of his actions. Is he guiding me? And so he is in me.

I find it ironic that this show was the last thing we did together, and that the ghost of the Simba's father realizes that his young cub has turned out exactly as he had planned. I get very sentimental when I reflect on all that has happened since Dad died. I miss him every day. They say that time heals. They say it just takes time. Who are these "they" anyway? Have "they" ever lost someone close? How long did "they" take to heal? How long is it supposed to take? I am still waiting. Everyone seems to have something to say, some opinion about the rules. But there are no rules. No predetermined way to deal with the grief. I will go days, weeks without so much as a tear. Then with no warning at all, I will see something or hear something, remember something about Dad, and the floodgates will open. The grief and sadness are just below the surface and are very overwhelming sometimes.

I am reminded daily as I live my life that the things I am doing, the choices I am making have been influenced in some way by his lessons and the way he lived his life. How can they not? I am his daughter. I can only be hopeful that I might be able to affect others in the same way that he did. Hopeful that the contributions I can make to this life will be half as great. Hopeful to hear that shout-out from the heavens as I reach goals, hit milestones, and accomplish new things.

Dad was certainly not a saint, although in my book, he came pretty close. He always taught Debbie and me to do our best. He gave us room to learn, room to make mistakes and then learn some more. I am not sure where it came from, but Dad always seemed to have this innate rule book. He always knew what to do and how do it, and he would do it right. Debbie and I would joke that even if he didn't know, he would just make something up. Even if that was the case, it always sounded right. At least to us. I am just trying to do my best and hopefully, some of the lessons are coming through so I can pass them on to my daughter.

It is now late August, and the garden we planted in early May has been producing all summer. We have been harvesting tomatoes, cucumbers, zucchini, and yellow squash. The experimental plants this summer were eggplant and watermelon. We always pick something we have never grown before just to try it and see what happens. I guess a little bit of the scientist is living on. The engineer in Dad would be asking me "How deep did you plant the seeds? How far apart? Did you give the plants room to grow and spread? How often do you water them?" As I stand out there each morning looking for the ripe vegetables to harvest, I can feel him. I talk to him. I keep waiting for the answers to come. He left us too soon. I'm still waiting for the healing part to start.

I am teaching my daughter, Everette, about gardening. She loves to just dig in the dirt. She helps to turn the soil and prepare it to grow vegetables. Then we plan what we will plant and plant everything in a precise way. Give each plant the room it needs to grow just like he taught me. And then you have to wait. Gardening is a great lesson in preparedness, discipline, and patience. Attributes my father had his whole life that he tried to instill in me and in others.

Once the plants start to sprout and grow, it is so exciting. The cucumbers pop out from the yellow flowers. Same for the tomatoes. The eggplant has a white blossom with a little bit of a lavender tint, similar to the purple fruit it will soon bear. We can't wait to watch everything grow day by day. When the vegetables are finally ready to pick, we take a basket to the garden and harvest all that we can.

Tomatoes and cucumbers ripen first. We make tomato sauce and tomato jam with the tomatoes. We make pickles with the cucumbers. We can them in mason jars. Preserve the vegetables and the sweet taste of summer. The watermelon is starting to grow, but it won't be ready to pick for a while. We can't wait to taste it, too. The taste of everything in the garden is just so much sweeter when you grow it yourself.

In January, when the ground is covered with snow and it's about twenty degrees outside, I will go to our pantry to get a jar of the tomato sauce we made or maybe grab a jar of the pickles. I will say to Everette, "See! We have summer in a jar!" Like so many years ago, as Sarah taught her children to do, and her child taught me, I am teaching mine. That's how the spirit lives on. It's how we preserve it.

Oliver's actions saved his children and preserved those lessons taught so many years ago. What he did allowed the traditions, the stories, the examples that we follow as a family today to carry on into tomorrow. I will make sure to savor every bite and savor all the memories. We preserve them, cherish them, and share them. That's how the lessons Dad was taught will live on. He shared them with me, showed me the way, and taught me. Just like the vegetables and fruit from the garden are saved in a jar, Dad will forever be saved and preserved in my heart.

Family Poetry

I don't remember how it got started, but for special events in our family, mostly birthdays and anniversaries, a poem was written to commemorate the occasion. It became a bit of a tradition for Debbie or me or both of us or sometimes Nicole to write a poem. Special birthdays or anniversaries always prompted us to write something lyrical that rhymed and to capture the moment. The poems gave a little more insight into Dad, our family, and the special bond we all shared.

Here are two of the poems that were written for two of Dad's special birthdays. Debbie and Nicole wrote one for Dad's sixtieth birthday. The second one we wrote for Dad's seventy-fifth birthday party. Humor and making one another laugh were just part of our everyday lives. Dad was always known for his sense of humor and making other people laugh. This was a way for us to give it back to him. Dad and Mom always enjoyed them. The guests who came to our family parties liked them, too. It was part of the tradition to hear us recite them at some point during a family celebration.

Pop-Pop
by Debbie Bogas and Nicole Bogas
(written February 1997)

On a cold winter day in '37,
Little James came down from heaven.
He was a bundle of joy.,
Let's hear it for the Birthday Boy!

His brothers and sisters numbered five.
At the house in Bowie they managed to thrive.
Then Fate stepped in, as she sometimes will,
And moved him out to old Sykesville!

Like Saving Summer in a Jar

The Strawbridge Home became the place
Where Jim and friends set the pace.
Sykesville High was thankful that
He came along to lead the pack!

As time went by, he found a date.
Her name was Lois, and she sure did rate!
After a while they were wed;,
As you can see, Lois kept Jim well fed!

A job he found at Martin Marietta.
The Space Race was on; it couldn't have been betta!!
The Race slowed down—almost to a stop.
To the Phone Company he did hop!

From Johns Hopkins U, he earned his degree.
His family was proud and so happy!
He now had time on the golf course to play.
"This is the life," he was heard to say!

Retirement came at an early age,
But Jim was not ready for this stage!
To Carroll Transit he took his smarts,
So senior citizens could get to Walmart!

To Debbie and Amy, he's known as Dad,
The very best one you could ever have!
He's always there no matter what.
The door to his heart is never shut!

Nicole and Allison call him Pop-Pop.
Their love for him will never stop-stop.

They have fun whenever they meet,
Even if they are not right across the street!

So here's to Jim: The country thanks him.
What he pays in taxes supports a small nation!
But he's happy to give and give and give—
That's just the kind of guy he is!

Three Cheers to Jim and Hip-Hip-Hooray.
Today is such a special day!
Happy Birthday to you and many more.
Your friends and family all are sure
They are glad to be here to celebrate.
You are sixty years young, and life is great!

The Birthday Boy! #75!
by Debbie Bogas and Amy Mathis
(written February 2012)

He was born James Oliver—
But what's in a name?
Jimmy, Dad, or Pop-Pop,
The great man is all the same!

Born in February 1937,
The first born of Oliver and Sarah,
Their little slice of heaven.

Fate would step in and change his course.
He was off to Sykesville to meet Lois, of course.
He was class President
At Sykesville High,
But he would soon be designing rockets
Meant to fly in the sky!

Jim and Lois wed in 1955,
And they are still together today
As they turn seventy-five!

First came Debbie
And Amy seven years later—
They girls were a joy,
Dancing, majorettes, music, and 4-H'ers!

Jim's days were filled with work,
His nights filled with school.
Off to Cate State and Hopkins he went
To become an educated Gent!

Amy Mathis

He went from outer space
To dividing Ma Bell,
To driving old people around
Whether at church, go with friends,
Breakfast with the ROMEOs...
He's still the man about town!

In a Baby Camper,
The family went off to OC.
On the family vacation they would be
We scratched and lit the citronella
And had nowhere to pee!

Who knew that this would be the start
Of their retirement dream?
Jim and Lois—the "campers"!
What an outdoorsy team

Jimmy is the oldest of six—
Sara, Richard, Ronnie, Inez, and Billy.
Today they are all over the country,
But when they get together, they are so silly!

The games they play, you wouldn't believe.
One Hung Low, Hen Party, and more—
Family Reunions, Strawbridge Reunions,
Lots of fun and laughs galore!

We are here to celebrate
A special birthday; ain't it great?
He's a Dad, a Husband,
A Brother, and a Friend.

To three girls he is Pop-Pop.
He's an engineer, a volunteer,
A driver, a student, a golfer,
And, some say, "Mr. Jiggle It"!
But today he is the Birthday Boy,
With seventy-five years to his credit!

Like the old cars that you love,
You are a classic, Dad!
And as we celebrate your special day,
We love you, are proud of you and
The great life you have had!

Seventy-five years young
Means there is lots more to come!
Let's all sing the birthday song
And get this party rolling along!

About the Author

AMY MATHIS WAS inspired by the life and work of her father, James "Jimmy" Mathis. She hopes that readers will receive similar encouragement from the story of his life and that it can inspire others to do the good works she and her family call "Jimmy deeds."

Mathis received her degree in business administration from Arcadia University, and she works in the financial services industry. She and her husband, Nick, have one daughter, Everette. They live near Philadelphia, Pennsylvania.

Made in the USA
Middletown, DE
15 September 2018